Facing our own brokenness, honestly confronting the wounded child within us, can be utterly excruciating. Johnny Honaker threaded his way through the pain to confront h__ inner hurt, and there he found the healing gr___ _____ free. Here is Honaker's bottom line _____ reat hope: there is no wound _____ not be healed.

, PHD

AUTHOR OF R_____ .DS TO CHANGE
YO ___LD, AND FIFTEEN OTHERS

Within the pages of this book, Pastor Johnny Honaker unveils a hidden internal enemy—brokenness. It shadows and robs us of our peace, our self-esteem, and our worth. We learn as we read that God's desire for us is not only to be free from our brokenness but also to take back what brokenness has confiscated. Pastor Johnny will teach you how to address your enemy. You will not walk away with empty hands; you will receive wholeness and God's gift of hope will swell within.

—PASTOR WILFREDO "CHOCO" DE JESÚS,
SENIOR PASTOR, NEW LIFE COVENANT CHURCH,
CHICAGO, ILLINOIS
TIME MAGAZINE'S "100 MOST INFLUENTIAL PEOPLE
IN THE WORLD," 2013
AUTHOR OF AMAZING FAITH, IN THE GAP,
AND STAY THE COURSE

Salvation is about so much more than getting people into heaven. It's about getting heaven into people. It's about restoring what has been lost and bringing healing and wholeness. Johnny Honaker's book *The Enemy in You* is a gift to the body of Christ that can unlock your God-given potential and change your life.

—DANIEL KOLENDA, MISSIONARY EVANGELIST
PRESIDENT AND CEO, CHRIST FOR ALL NATIONS

Every person experiences times of pain and brokenness. No one is immune; it's part of the human condition. It's easy to enter a season like this and become trapped. If you or someone you love is facing this dilemma, you're holding hope in your hands. Pastor Johnny Honaker has written a book dripping with encouragement and instruction. With the turning of each page, the reader will discover the life keys for moving from pain to power and from brokenness to breakthrough.

—JIM RALEY, PASTOR
CALVARY CHRISTIAN CENTER, ORMOND BEACH, FLORIDA
AUTHOR OF HELL'S SPELLS AND DREAM KILLERS

Every person breathing air on this planet has been blessed with the seed of greatness. Unfortunately, the majority of people have either never heard this truth or have been deceived by the greatest lie ever told to mankind: "You can't be great." The most difficult truth to embrace on the journey to greatness is that the only real enemy of destiny is the one we look at in the mirror every day. To fulfill your dreams and goals, "the enemy in you" has got to be dealt with! This book will help you navigate the trouble within and find healing and wholeness and unlock your potential into greatness. Pastor Honaker shows you that your best days are ahead and your healing is at hand.

—SHANE WARREN, LEAD PASTOR
THE ASSEMBLY, WEST MONROE, LOUISIANA
AUTHOR OF THE LAST DAYS OF AMERICA?,
UNLOCKING THE HEAVENS, AND THE IDEAL LIFE

The Enemy in You is an eye-opening study revealing the potential of Holy Spirit power to effect deliverance and healing in believers' lives. Johnny Honaker rightly addresses inner hurt, grief, and regret experienced by believers from varying backgrounds and experiences without interruption even after receiving Jesus Christ as Savior. The believer will identify with some if not all the vehicles Satan uses to keep the believer in bondage and hopelessness. Honaker encourages the believer's right to hope: healing and freedom from the wounds of life through application of specific and practical scriptural principles. These practical steps toward a healed and healthy Christian life are helpful and life changing.

I heartily endorse *The Enemy in You*. You will not be able to put it down. You will find yourself coming back to it again and again.

—DAVID STOCKER, PASTOR
CALVARY ASSEMBLY OF GOD, ORANGE PARK, FLORIDA

With pastoral compassion and prophetic insight, Pastor Johnny Honaker leads his readers on a journey of personal discovery and defeat of "the enemy within." Your journey begins now.

—FRANK P. ADAMS, PASTOR, AUTHOR,
LEADERSHIP COACH

With unmistakable clarity, Pastor Johnny Honaker offers hope to all of us who have ever been wounded. Drawing from his own experience as a pastor and follower of Christ, he reminds us that God can take mistakes, tragedy, and even the most painful events we go through and redeem them and use them to produce a vessel for His glory. Wholeness is possible! From brokenness to blessings, from pain to purpose, from a mess to a message, God will always have the last word. This book is one of those you will read time and again and want to pass on to others.

—MARK L. WILLIAMS, LEAD PASTOR
NORTH CLEVELAND CHURCH OF GOD
GENERAL OVERSEER, CHURCH OF GOD, 2012–2016

Since the fall of man in the Garden of Eden, when fig leaves were woven together to cover what the eye could see, human nature will always attempt to hide the real issue of the heart. This book will open the windows of your soul and bring to light a new freedom to experience life from God's perspective.

—TOMMY BATES, PASTOR
INDEPENDENCE, KENTUCKY

This powerful book spoke to me as a CEO who has experienced success after many failures both professionally and personally. Pastor Honaker exposes the truth of how staying broken will hinder God's best in our lives. This is a book of great inspiration, courage, and hope; every word rings with truth, purpose, and the passion of someone who has experienced restoring power.

—David Villa, CEO, IPD

It is a joy to commend the excellent ministry manuscript of my friend, Pastor Johnny Honaker. His book, *The Enemy in You: Journey from Brokenness to Wholeness*, offers help and hope to all of us who have been wounded and scarred by life. He fearlessly identifies the enemies that keep us bound in discouragement and defeat and, more importantly, provides practical and biblical instruction that guides toward wholeness in soul, mind, and body. Anyone and everyone can benefit from *The Enemy in You*! In Pastor Johnny's own words: "Never forget that the cross was followed by a resurrection." Amen!

—Terry Raburn, Superintendent
Peninsular Florida District Council
of the Assemblies of God

Johnny Honaker is a merchant of hope. He gives hope to everyone he meets. His new book is filled with hope for restoration, recovery, and re-starting. I think you will feel as though Pastor Johnny is talking straight to your heart as he did to mine. The enemy within you will be replaced with a wheelbarrow full of hope.

—Dr. Steve Greene, Charisma Media Publisher
and Executive Vice President—Media Group

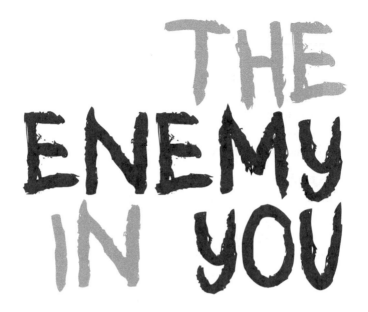

THE ENEMY IN YOU

JOURNEY FROM BROKENNESS TO WHOLENESS

JOHNNY HONAKER

CREATION
HOUSE

THE ENEMY IN YOU: JOURNEY FROM BROKENNESS TO
WHOLENESS
by Johnny Honaker
Published by Creation House
A Charisma Media Company
600 Rinehart Road
Lake Mary, Florida 32746
www.charismamedia.com

by permission of Tyndale House Publishers, Inc., Wheaton, IL 60189. All rights reserved.

Cover design by Jon Minuto

Visit the author's website: TheEnemyInYou.com

Library of Congress Control Number: 2017940143
International Standard Book Number: 978-1-62999-215-0
E-book International Standard Book Number:
978-1-62999-216-7

While the author has made every effort to provide accurate telephone numbers and Internet addresses at the time of publication, neither the publisher nor the author assumes any responsibility for errors or for changes that occur after publication.

First edition

17 18 19 20 21— 987654321
Printed in the United States of America

This book is dedicated to the broken and hurting, the wounded and rejected, the silent sufferers who hide in pulpits and corner offices with their name on the door. This book has a message that will lead you on a journey from brokenness to wholeness and emotional healthiness.

I have prayed for you as I have written this book; a prayer for God to bring healing to every hurt and broken place in your life. This book is a hand that is extended to those who feel lost and forgotten in the brokenness of their stories. Your wounds are going to heal and become whole. From your scars will come a story to aid in the healing of others. You will discover that Jesus glows in the dark places of your life and that broken crayons get to color.

CONTENTS

Foreword xiii

Acknowledgments xvii

Introduction xxi

Chapter 1: The Dark Side 1

Chapter 2: Purpose in Pain 9

Chapter 3: Tear Down These Walls 25

Chapter 4: Reinforced Walls 39

Chapter 5: Scarlet Letter 55

Chapter 6: Potter's Field 71

Chapter 7: Snake Bitten 87

Chapter 8: Collateral Damage 99

Chapter 9: The Judas Goat 111

Chapter 10: Orphan Spirit 123

Chapter 11: Journey to Wholeness 137

Chapter 12: Right as Rain 149

Notes 163

About the Author 179

Contact the Author 181

you have survived to bring praise to God. God will use only those who start their testimony with: "If it had not been for Jesus...."

There are no overnight successes! There are just those who made a decision to be an overcomer regardless of what they have faced. What you have been through is a great indication of who you are called to. What the enemy would love to use to disqualify is actually what God will use to engineer a life of victory. God will set you aside for His purpose and even hide you in a cave to get your attention. It is when you die to self that God resurrects you for His purpose. This is when you realize that every aspect of your past can become a part of your purpose! We cannot be victims of yesterday but must be revisionists of our today. You were not created to live looking in the rearview mirror but to move forward in victory.

The book *The Enemy in You* has taught me that if God can transform my thinking then I can be His hands and feet to the hurting. You will feel stirred to take back the second half of your life. Johnny teaches us that "true champions emerge in the second half" and that you will "have a fourth quarter that someone will write about." As you read this book you will receive a mandate from heaven that God is a God of second chances and an enabler of lost causes!

Maybe you have lived in anonymity and it seems as if the world has passed you by. You will soon understand that the greater the anointing the greater the isolation. God was preparing you for now! You are the one who God has been waiting to use to rescue the hurting, rejuvenate the living, and revive the religious.

Thank you to my friend Johnny for writing this powerful book. *The Enemy in You* is a game changer for those ready to arise and lead! It is time to take back what the enemy stole! This is your now!

—Patrick Schatzline, Evangelist and Author
Remnant Ministries International

ACKNOWLEDGMENTS

To JOHN WESLEY and Ashland, Casey and Jon: Words fail to express the gratitude and love that I have for each of you. Your encouragement has caused me to reach higher and trust deeper. I pray that the dreams God has placed in you become a reality. Settle for nothing less than the Designer's original for your life. Release the gifts on the inside of you and let the world know you have been here. Trust your pain and allow it to guide you to Jesus. He has been proven to be trustworthy with the messy parts of life. Together we have skinned our hearts and skinned our knees, but we have always believed and supported each other. My love for you is unfailing, and remember that I will always be your biggest fan.

To my mother: Your relentless sacrifice and selflessness has not gone unnoticed. Your love is not just spoken but demonstrated. Your faith and love for Jesus is the purest I have ever witnessed. Your prayers are trusted and your guidance is heeded. In a world where there is a scramble for accolades and titles, the one that you have desired and earned above all is that of a mother. The loving arms that held a frightened little boy on a stormy night on a front porch swing are the same that have comforted and encouraged throughout the years. Know that I love and cherish you with all my heart.

Carl: Thank you for being a part of our family and most of all for loving my mother. When my father passed away I could not imagine my mother ever being with anyone else, but I am so very grateful that He sent you into her life and ours. You are a man of great integrity and character with a heart of gold. I am proud to call you father.

To my dad: You are in heaven awaiting the arrival of your family. If you were here with me, what I would choose to say to you is: Dad, it is not your brokenness that I remember, and all that sat at King David's table had brokenness. It wasn't just Mephibosheth that was broken. I remember your hands that were afraid to discipline me but not to love and protect me, your hands that provided for me and taught me work ethic, your hands as they applauded the swing of a bat in little league and the first message when God called me to preach, your hands that would hold my son as you once held me, your hands that would hold tightly the hand of my mother and would not let go, your hands as they would fold in prayer as Jesus would begin to make you whole. Dad, with you as an inspiration, my hands hold tightly to the baton and I will finish the race strong.

To my friends and mentors and those who have shared in vision with me: Thank you to those that looked past my brokenness and saw something in me that I could not see in myself. To my mentors, thank you not only for your instruction but for loving me enough to offer a rebuke when it was necessary. Thank you for allowing me to serve in your fields till God would summon me to my position and purpose. Thank you for access to acquire from your strengths and for trusting me to learn from your vulnerabilities. Thank you for those who did not give up on me when I spilled my insecurities on your life and ministry. To each of you I am forever grateful for your contribution and investment in my life and ministry. Thank you for allowing me to make deposits in you that are sure to reap kingdom returns.

To my teen crush and sweetheart and love of my life, CC: What you have meant to me is more difficult to express than any of the chapters I have written in this book. How do you say thank you to someone that has meant so much? No one's applause has been louder and meant more. The affirmation and confidence that you have given has inspired and encouraged me to never settle for mediocrity. I am a better man and person because I have you in my life. You have been a safe place for me to rest my head when there were boos from my brokenness. You are my left tackle and have stood humbly beside me while I have been celebrated from the stands. But I know there are no touchdowns or wins in my life without you. You are a true woman of God, and your loyalty and friendship is unmatched. After all of the years and life that we have shared, you are still the one that turns my head. You are my very best friend and I love you and always will.

INTRODUCTION

D R. MARK RUTLAND is a man whom I hold in high
regard and respect greatly. I came across an article
published in *Charisma Magazine* by Dr. Rutland
that has influenced and changed my life. The article is
titled "Ten Things I Wish I'd Known When I Was 21." It
is number one on a list of ten that God used to speak into
my life. Dr. Rutland writes the following:

> It is probably impossible to arrive at 21, let alone
> 64, without wounds in the inner person—deep
> wounds that need God's healing grace. The
> more I see of inner healing and the more I face
> up to my own inner wounds, the more I wish
> I had let the Messiah touch my deepest hurts
> earlier in life. That childhood hurt, that hidden
> outrage, that long-suppressed horrific memory
> can lurk like a monster in the basement waiting
> for years, even decades, to rise and wreak havoc.
> Hiding the monster, denying that it's down
> there, is a dangerous game. The temptation is to
> create an alternative reality where success and
> accomplishment and appearances seem so very
> real and the monster but a mirage. If I were 21
> again I would bore down into the inner world of
> me and find Christ's healing touch in the darkness
> under the floorboards.[1]

As I read the honesty and vulnerability of someone whom I look up to and respect greatly, I was encouraged to do just what the article suggested. I began to look deep inside myself to search out the brokenness that was hiding in my insecurities and behaviors. How many times have I asked myself, "Why did I respond that way? Where did that come from? That is not who I am." I witnessed my brokenness manifesting itself through insecurities in my leadership and other places that God had trusted me to influence. I used manipulation and aggressive words to control my environment and to camouflage the weaknesses in my life. I lashed out and attacked anything and anyone whom I considered a threat and an enemy except for the enemy that was in me. I discovered that, although I loved Jesus and was serving Him with all of my heart and He was blessing my life, there was brokenness in me that He wanted to address and make whole. At the dawning of this realization, my journey from brokenness to wholeness would begin.

TREASON FROM WITHIN

The most dangerous enemies of America are those that live within our borders. The enemy that has the highest potential of harming our nation is the one that is homegrown, lives among us, is educated in our universities, commingles in the American dream, shows up at Christmas parties, and works the security of gated communities with evil plots of destruction in mind. Marcus Tullius Cicero, the great Roman philosopher, statesman, and lawyer, stated the following:

> A nation can survive its fools, and even the ambitious. But it cannot survive treason from within. An enemy at the gates is less formidable, for he is known and carries his banner openly. But the traitor moves amongst those within the gate freely, his sly whispers rustling through all the

alleys, heard in the very halls of government itself. For the traitor appears not a traitor; he speaks in accents familiar to his victims, and he wears their face and their arguments, he appeals to the baseness that lies deep in the hearts of all men. He rots the soul of a nation, he works secretly and unknown in the night to undermine the pillars of the city, he infects the body politic so that it can no longer resist. A murderer is less to fear.[2]

When the enemy penetrates the borders of your heart through the entry gate of your calamity and brokenness, it becomes destructive and dangerous. It is the poison and ill effects of what bit you that lie deep within, undermining the pillars of your purpose. The Judas goat has secretly infected you, moving freely within, slyly whispering, and rustling through the alleys of your emotions. It is the enemy in you that will prove to be your fiercest adversary.

EMPTY-HANDED

In 1 Samuel 30, David and his mighty men were out fighting battles on other fronts. While engaged in battle on one front, his home and family were left vulnerable and unprotected. The Ammonite enemy had invaded Ziklag, burned David's home to the ground, and taken his wives, children, and livestock. As David sat among the ashes of Ziklag, God spoke to him and told him to go and pursue his enemy, defeat them, and recover all that he had lost (vv. 1–8).

In Exodus 3, God spoke to Moses and said that His people had been held captive by Pharaoh and the Egyptians for 430 years. Moses was to go to Pharaoh and tell him to set His people free (vv. 7–10). Over a course of miraculous events, Pharaoh tells Moses the Israelites can go but commands that their sons, daughters, and livestock be left in Egypt (10:10). Moses is reminded of God's promise that the Israelites would not leave Egypt empty-handed (3:21). So Moses tells Pharaoh, "We're coming out of Egypt, and we're taking our families with us" (10:9). In Exodus 12, we read that the Israelites left with their hands full. They left with their sons and their daughters, with gold and silver, and with clothing and livestock (vv. 35–38).

When David went into the enemy's camp and defeated the Ammonites, he recovered everything and left nothing; he came out with his hands full (1 Sam. 30:19–20). Everything that had been plundered from David was recovered.

You have fought battles and had many calamities in your life. The storm is over and God has given you many victories, but you have yet to recover what was plundered from you. You were delivered from the oppression of what enslaved you, but your joy and peace were left in Egypt. Your self-worth was left in the wreckage of your calamity. There is no evidence of a victory. You walked out of your battle empty-handed. You went into the enemy's camp and defeated the adversary but have yet to recover what was stolen from you. Your purpose was left in the Ammonite camp because you were convinced that you were no longer worthy of what had been taken from you. There are ministries, great dreams, and visions that have been left in Egypt; families and relationships that have never been recovered remain in the ruins and ashes of the battlefield.

In your journey from brokenness to wholeness, God will bring healing and wholeness to your life and you will ascend from the ashes and ruins to recover the treasure that was lost in your pain and calamity.

DO YOU WANT TO BE WHOLE?

John 5:1–9 tells us of when Jesus visited the pool of Bethesda. All around the basin there were people who were sick and broken. It was at this place that Jesus would speak to a man who had been broken for thirty-eight years. Jesus did not ask the man if he wanted to be healed because the man needed more than just healing. In thirty-eight years of brokenness, there was much that had been taken from this man. His self-worth and value had been replaced with insecurities and low self-esteem. His purpose and dream had faded over the years, a result of the crippling effect of his dysfunction. Jesus asked the man if he wanted to be whole (v. 6, KJV). Thirty-eight years of brokenness in this man had created emotional instabilities. Jesus saw past his obvious need and addressed the internal enemy that was inside of him by asking, "Do you want to be made whole?" It is the question that is asked of you as you begin to read this book. Do you want to be made whole? Don't put this book down until you allow the Holy Spirit to identify and confront the brokenness in your life and lead you on a journey to wholeness. As you allow the Holy Spirit to navigate you through the pain of your brokenness, you will recover all that the enemy stole from you. You will find wholeness and walk out with your hands full.

CHAPTER 1

THE DARK SIDE

Man is like the moon, and has a dark side
which he never shows to anybody.[1]
—MARK TWAIN

M ARK TWAIN SAID about depravity that we are all like the moon; we have a dark side we don't want anyone to see. The dark side is that part of you that you don't talk about. The dark side is the part of your testimony that has yet to be heard. The dark side does not show up on resumes or in funeral eulogies, but we all have one.

Hollywood has made millions on the thought of confronting the dark side; from *Star Wars* to *Spiderman* it has exploited the brokenness of human nature. The rock band Pink Floyd released the album *The Dark Side of the Moon* in 1973 and the album would remain on the Billboard chart for 741 weeks and would sell 45 million copies and ranks as one of the greatest albums of all time.[2] The dark side may sell albums and movies, but it is that which man finds difficult to address in his life.

The dark side is that painful reminder of the brokenness of humanity—the secrets that haunt from the basement of your life. When you think of the dark side, you often think of some hidden or secret sin that you don't want anyone to know. But that is not always the case; brokenness has many entry points: the wounds of hateful words spoken in anger, the rejection experienced by a child of an absentee parent, the shame of failure, the betrayal of trust. Its arsenal of weapons continues as each painful experience chips away at the wholeness of the soul. To ignore what has happened in your life does not make it go away. The things that you refuse to acknowledge and address do not just vanish and never reappear. Rather, from the dark side they continue to show up at different places and different seasons, wreaking havoc and dysfunction in God's purpose and His plan for your life.

As you continue on the journey to spiritual maturity and wholeness, the more aware you will become of your own brokenness. It will become evident that you have been incorrectly identifying your enemies. The enemy that serves as your greatest threat is the enemy in you.

The old proverb says better the devil you know than the devil you don't know. It is the enemy within you that has penetrated your walls and has taken possession of your identity and self-worth.

The journey to wholeness is a painful road delayed by your pride and stubbornness. It is the enemy of self-deception that serves as your greatest hindrance. Self-deception can prove to be your worst deception in that you cannot confront and conquer an enemy that you refuse to identify.

WHO TOLD YOU THAT YOU WERE NAKED?

Think of the purity and innocence of a baby. There is no awareness of its own nakedness. It has a heart that has never known hurt, never felt the ugliness of jealousy, never known bitterness, never felt guilt and shame, or never experienced demobilizing fear. At what point does the heart stop trusting? At what point does the heart empty itself of the dreams that once burned with passion? At what point does the heart start to believe it is not good enough?

In the first two chapters of Genesis, Adam and Eve had not

yet experienced the dark side. They had not yet experienced the weight of their brokenness. All they had known was paradise, experiencing only perfect fellowship with God. In Genesis chapter 3, humanity would be introduced to the dark side! The first family, Adam and Eve, experienced the same pleasures of an innocent child having never experienced the brokenness that creates the dark places. The first man had never been confronted with the erratic behavior of insecurities. The first couple did not know what jealousy in a relationship felt like; their relationship had only known trust. For a child, the dark side is usually a slow accumulation of damage and injury that grows to an unmanageable amount of baggage, but with Adam and Eve it would happen suddenly with one bite.

In Genesis 3:7, the tragic events unfold. Can you imagine at that moment, with one bite, paradise was lost? Adam and Eve, for the first time, would get a glimpse of the dark side. Suddenly their eyes would be opened, and there would be an awareness of their own nakedness, an awareness of their own brokenness. Their response to the dark side was to look for a covering. Humanity's answer for the dark side has not changed, in that man still searches for a covering for the brokenness he refuses to confront. Oh, the horror of that moment! I can only imagine what it must have been like for the first family. Emotions that they had never experienced suddenly, with one bite, became a gruesome reality: shame for the first time, guilt for the first time. Fear and insecurity would introduce themselves and bring Adam and Eve face-to-face with the dark side. Blame and manipulation were introduced to humanity, along with behaviors that they never knew existed. At that moment fear was born into this perfect world that God had created. Fear and insecurity that would wreak havoc in countless lives; tearing apart families and marriages, ruining ministries, and dividing churches while attacking dreams and anything that resembled potential.

This brokenness would have the first family pulling leaves from the garden to cover themselves.

In Genesis 3:11, God arrived and asked the question, "Who told you that you were naked?" The first family hears God approaching, and for the first time humanity takes their brokenness and runs from Him. God never asks questions to gain information. God is drawing attention to the brokenness within them. We see the failed attempt of Adam to hide and cover up his brokenness as God calls from the garden, "Who told you that you were naked?" God calls so loud that it is heard thousands of years into the future. To the successful businessman He says, "Who told you that you were naked?" To the single mom He says, "Who told you that you were naked?" To the pastor He says, "Who told you that you were naked?" God is not asking the question to gather information but to help you identify the brokenness that is within you to bring you to a place of wholeness.

THE DARK SIDE OF THE MOON

According to scientists, 59 percent of the moon is visible from the earth over the course of an orbit. Forty-one percent of the moon you never see, the side they call the dark side.[3] Most people only see 59 percent of you; there is another 41 percent that remains in the dark. You can be married to someone for years but only have met 59 percent of who they are. You have become curious and tried to open the door into the basement of the dark side of your spouse, but you have only been formally introduced to 59 percent of the one you married and now is the father or the mother of your children. The 41 percent is the accumulation of the insecurities, brokenness, and dysfunctions of life that also make up the dark side in you.

I met my wife on a church bus, a ministry of a country church. My first memory of her was staring out the window as the bus drove up in front of her humble wood-frame house. The curly headed, chubby girl with the broken arm boarded the bus as her mother waved from the front steps. The brief encounter on the old blue church bus would play a significant role in both of our lives. The summer of the year that I graduated from high school, a beautiful young woman—who resembled the curly headed chubby girl with the broken arm from the old blue church bus—walked back into my life. We began a relationship that would lead to thirty years of marriage and two beautiful children and a ministry that we would partner and share together. My wife fell in love with the 59 percent of me that I introduced to her, and I fell deeply in love with the 59 percent of her with which I had become acquainted. When our love was young, either the 59 percent was enough or we were blinded to the fact that there was another 41 percent to which we had not formally been introduced.

On August 1, 1987, my wife and I were married. Together we stood at the altar of the church where I was serving as a youth pastor. As we exchanged our vows, I looked into her eyes and I said "I do," and she looked back into my eyes with the innocence of her youth and said "I do." With the words "I do" we not only pledged our love to the 59 percent known but also committed ourselves to the 41 percent that had silenced itself in the holiness of the moment. The 41 percent made surprise visits during the courtship but in the immaturity of young love was ignored. In all of the preparations and planning that goes into the big day, what has a tendency not to make it on the to-do list is the need to address the dark side.

If I had known what I have painfully come to realize, I would have identified and addressed the dark side in me before being married. I would have cried out to the Lord for His wholeness and healing. I would have addressed the broken things within me that were sure to surface at some point in our marriage. Through the years, though still not formally introduced, we would become more familiar with the 41 percent of the dark side that was kept hidden in the basement deep inside our lives—the 41 percent that was beginning to make more and more appearances through outbursts and dysfunctional behaviors. It would be the Lord and our love of the 59 percent that would keep us faithful to the vow that we committed to each other. As we moved away from the honeymoon season of our marriage, the 41 percent—the dark side, the brokenness and insecurities— though still not formally introduced, was drawing more of an audience from our feelings and emotions.

The 59 percent was discovering that it was not as effective as it had been in the past in covering up for the damage that had been caused by the dark side. The promises and apologies were getting weaker and not as effective as they once were. Though sincere, "I'm sorry" and the promises of corrected behavior would only be temporary. Though not formally introduced, we were getting to know the other 41 percent in each other quite well; in fact, she was getting to know my 41 percent better than I did.

It was the hiding of the 41 percent that would create a loneliness and vulnerability in my wife—the 41 percent of me that wouldn't talk; the 41 percent that was not meeting a need in the wife whom God had given me.

In the marriage of the first couple, Adam and Eve, we witness what is necessary for a relationship to be healthy and whole. Genesis 2:25 says that the first couple, Adam and his wife, Eve, were naked and not ashamed (KJV). As I look deep into the context of this verse, I have come to realize that the nakedness of Adam and Eve was not just that they realized the need for clothing. I see the nakedness, the honesty and vulnerability that is necessary for a relationship to be strong and healthy. The brokenness in the 41 percent would not allow me to get emotionally naked with my wife. For many couples it is not difficult to see the threat and the problem that is caused when there is no nakedness in the physical, but we are blinded to the vulnerable state of a marriage that is absent of emotional nakedness.

Broken men still have a sex drive.

Many of the men I have spoken with and given counsel have expressed frustration with the lack of nakedness and sex in their marriage. There may have been evidence of brokenness in their lives, but their sex drive was still very much intact. They would attack their wife and belittle her for the lack of physical nakedness using such tactics as guilt, the fear of betrayal, and if necessary the use of selective biblical scriptures. Often these manipulated wives give in to the tactics of the husbands whom they love and settle for sex as their soul cries out for intimacy.

I understand the need and the importance of meeting the sexual needs of your spouse, but equally important is the meeting of the need for emotional nakedness.

The same men that expressed frustration over the absence of sexual nakedness could not see the hurt in their wife when it came to her need for emotional nakedness.

Broken men make broken husbands.

I would discover that a broken man made for a broken husband. The dysfunctional behaviors and insecurities that stemmed from the broken places in my life would not be prejudiced in where they would choose to manifest. Insecurities would surface from my dark side and would affect my decisions and judgment in every area of my life and ministry. The brokenness in me would produce a broken husband. My wife's need for emotional nakedness was apparent, but the brokenness and dysfunction within prevented me from giving her what she desperately needed.

I wanted to open my heart and give her what she needed, but the dysfunction from my dark side prevented me from doing so. I was a broken man that made for a broken husband that was creating a broken marriage. I am writing from the perspective of a man and husband, but it is certain that a broken woman makes for a broken wife that contributes to a broken marriage as well.

Whole men make whole husbands.

Broken people can achieve and be highly successful. Broken men can be gifted and have a strong work ethic. Broken women can possess great talents and skills. God can and has anointed broken people. I preached some of my best messages after episodes of outburst from the broken places in my life. Something I have learned is that we must never mistake God's grace as approval of the brokenness in our lives. Never confuse God's anointing on His Word for the acceptance of the things that are destroying His children. The growth of our churches and ministry and success in the corporate world can draw attention away from our need for wholeness. God refuses to accept the credentials of the things that we have learned and accomplished while dismissing the areas that need to be healed and made whole. Corporate successes and wall plaques will not silence the voices from the dark side. The insecurities on the inside of you will sit down for a moment only to reappear with a louder and stronger presence than ever before.

The journey from brokenness to wholeness in your life will allow you to become more effective in each of the places where the dark side has shown its face. It is because of God's healing and wholeness in your life that you will become a stronger man or a stronger woman, a better husband or a better wife. Broken men make broken husbands, but whole men make whole husbands. Broken women make broken wives, but women that are whole make wives that are whole.

CHAPTER 2

PURPOSE IN PAIN

*In some ways suffering ceases to be suffering
at the moment that it finds a meaning.[1]*
—VIKTOR FRANKL

IF YOU DON'T understand the purpose of pain, you are rejecting one of your closest allies in the battle for wholeness. Emotional and psychological pain, which at times is less dramatic than physical pain, can be more common and more difficult to bear. An individual mugged and beaten has wounds that cannot be easily hidden or ignored. Unfortunately, emotional trauma is easy to disguise. There is no outward bleeding, although the soul is hemorrhaging. Any attempt to conceal and hide emotional pain only increases the burden.

C. S. Lewis said, "It is easier to say 'My tooth is aching' than to say 'My heart is broken.'"[2]

Often we attempt to deal with emotional trauma through substance abuse therapy and prescription medications. Pain that is misunderstood causes you to drive down dark streets on the seedy side of town. You find yourself purchasing from a car window, which only gives a moment of relief from your haunting reality that will not leave you alone. Pain without purpose will leave you unemployed, isolated, and alone. Pain that is misunderstood causes dysfunctional behaviors that leave you scarred and labeled: drunk, addict, whore, cheat, liar, manipulator, and loser. Your soul is then branded with the white-hot iron of your brokenness and failures; it is pain that grieves for your true identity.

Pain is not prejudice. It cares not the color of your skin or your economic status. Pain visits both sides of the tracks—the haves, and the have-nots. Both sides will find the loyalty of its presence. Pain that is ignored, numbed, and blocked will momentarily disappear only to reappear more ferocious in the quest for wholeness. The tendency is to view pain as the enemy, causing a misunderstanding of its real purpose. Don't shoot the messenger and avoid the message. The message of pain is evident and its purpose direct. Pain alerts the body to a wound that needs healing. Pain is not enjoyed or appreciated, but necessary in diagnosing and healing of the injury. Only after the Holy Spirit navigates you through the process of brokenness to wholeness, then and only then do you value pain's purpose. It is only after healing that you can appreciate pain's relentless push to wholeness. Your pain has been assigned to bring you to wholeness. Your pain asks the hard questions to determine your diagnosis. Your pain demands an explanation of behaviors. Pain is OK with not being considered your friend, but its commitment is without question. It will not leave you till it has been satisfied. Its satisfaction is not in your misery, nor is it in the river of your tears. Pain's satisfaction comes from your wholeness and healing from the broken places of your life. Pain's greatest reward is its partnership with your purpose—a partnership that not only brings you to wholeness but brings healing to your relationships as well.

In the book *Man's Search for Meaning*, Viktor Frankl reveals his search for the purpose in the pain he endured at the hands of the Nazis. Viktor was a medical doctor from Vienna. In 1941, he married Tilly Grosser. After only one year of marriage, they would be arrested by the Nazis, forced to abort their unborn child, and sent to a concentration camp. Needless to say, the newlyweds had experienced an insurmountable amount of pain in their short married life. After spending three years in inhumane and deplorable conditions, Viktor was finally set free from the Nazi concentration camp, only to return home to discover the heartbreaking news that his wife and family were dead. How is it that a person who has experienced such loss can produce so much good? After surviving the Nazi concentration camp and the heartbreaking loss of his family, Viktor Frankl would go on to write thirty-nine books, receive twenty-nine honorary doctorates, and teach at four universities.[3] Viktor Frankl answered the question when he wrote, "Suffering ceases to be suffering in some way in the moment that it finds a meaning."[4] When you realize that the discomfort of your pain is actually working for you and not against you, then you begin to reap the benefits and discover the purpose from the pain that you have endured.

Producing Pearls

A pearl is formed when a foreign substance makes its way into the tight seal of an oyster's shell. As a natural defense mechanism against the irritant, the oyster produces the fluid nacre, which envelops the intruder and prevents further damage. Layer upon layer the nacre is deposited, creating a beautiful pearl.[5] When an oyster is harvested from the bottom of the ocean and a pearl is revealed, others see its beauty; but the oyster sees great suffering. An oyster that has never known brokenness and experienced pain cannot produce pearls. A pearl is the result of an oyster's brokenness that has become whole. The pain from the broken places of your life can be so intense you can't see how anything good could ever come from such darkness. Suffering has a way of blinding you to everything and anything beyond the pain of your current circumstances. Viktor Frankl could identify with suffering. He had experienced more than most. In the midst of his grief, Viktor Frankl chose to look for the purpose in his pain and produce pearls of wisdom he would share with generations to follow.

Victor Goertzel, the president of an organization dealing with gifted students, and Mildred Goertzel, director of an institution dealing with emotionally disturbed children, began research on the qualities that set people apart. Their question was what the key component was that stood out about men and women who had accomplished great things and made a name for themselves. They studied the lives of 413 "famous and exceptionally gifted people."[6] They were attempting to understand what produced such greatness that set them apart. What produces the pearls in their lives? Were there things that each of these men and women had in common? In 1962, they published their findings in a book entitled *Cradles of Eminence*.[7] One common experience that each of those well-accomplished individuals shared was that each had suffered greatly in their lives; 392 of the 413 admitted to having experienced suffering.[8] There was brokenness and pain in each of their lives. Each of the 392 famous individuals had made the journey from brokenness to wholeness.

CRUSHING OF THE OLIVE

Your brokenness can feel like you are being crushed. To be crushed, pressure has to be applied. The greater the pressure that is applied, the greater the crushing that takes place. The pressure and the pain may seem unbearable, but God is bringing you to a place of wholeness. What the pearl is to the oyster, the oil of God's anointing will be in your life. It is the men and women that have experienced much pain and brokenness that God uses the greatest. It is from your suffering that you will produce oil.

God's grace is freely given, but His anointing is costly. Oil in the Scriptures is symbolic of the anointing. The brokenness of the oyster at wholeness produces a pearl. The brokenness of God's men and women at wholeness produces oil, the oil of the anointing.

God's great men and women are those who have visited Gethsemane. Gethsemane is derived from Hebrew words meaning "oil press."[9] Pressure is applied to the olives, and it is the crushing of the olives that produces the oil; the more pressure, the more oil. As you search the Scriptures, you will find that many of the men and women whom God used in a significant way went through a crushing. If you were to think right now of your favorite Bible character, you could identify a place of crushing in their life.

The men and women who have become God's voice to the nations are those that have been to Gethsemane to the crushing floor. There has been a crushing of the olives in their life. Remember: the greater the pressure, the greater the oil of His anointing. To those who are experiencing an unexplainable amount of hurt and brokenness, who are feeling unbearable pressure, who are dealing with pain that is exceeding your threshold, and who have not been able to find the purpose in that pain, your brokenness is coming to a place of wholeness and God is sending an increase of His anointing upon your life.

As you continue to read this book, what has kept you in the darkness will be exposed. You will see yourself in Gethsemane; you will sense the anointing increase upon your life. The Lord will reveal His purpose that will come out of the pain, brokenness, and dysfunction that found you early in life. The enemy is intimidated by the potential and purpose that God has placed in you that is waiting to be released upon the world.

REDEMPTIVE PAIN

> Other people are going to find healing in your
> wounds. Your greatest life messages and your
> most effective ministry will come out of your
> deepest hurts.[10]
>
> —RICK WARREN

Redemptive pain takes place when God turns your mess into a message. It's your journey from brokenness to wholeness that is paving a road for others. God never wastes a hurt! He uses your pain. He uses your suffering. The thing you're most ashamed of in your life that brought you the most pain could become your greatest ministry in helping other people. It is often through your pain that you discover God's purpose.

Elisa Morgan served as president of MOPS (Mothers of Preschoolers). Under her leadership, MOPS grew from 350 to over 4,000 groups in the United States and an additional thirty countries. MOPS reaches over 1,000,000 mothers who are served and encouraged every year.[11] Morgan would have been the least likely candidate to lead such an organization. She endured much pain as a little girl and grew up in a broken home. The job of being a mother was never properly modeled for her. God brought wholeness into Elisa's life when she was a young woman. He did not allow Elisa's pain to be wasted but instead redeemed it to use her in a powerful way.

In her testimony Elisa shares:

> I'm probably the least likely person to head a
> mothering organization that impacts thousands
> of mothers' lives for the gospel. I grew up in a
> broken home. My parents were divorced when I
> was five. My older sister, younger brother and I
> were raised by my alcoholic mother. While my
> mother meant well, most of my memories are of

my mothering her, rather than her mothering me. Alcohol altered her love. I remember her weaving down the hall of our ranch home in Houston, Texas, glass of scotch in hand. I would wake her at seven each morning to try to get her off to work. Ten years ago, when I was asked to consider leading MOPS International, a vital ministry that nurtures mothers, I went straight to my knees. How could God use me—who had never been mothered—to nurture other mothers? The answer came, "My grace is sufficient for you, for my power is made perfect in weakness" (2 Corinthians 12:9, NIV). God would take my deficits and make them my offering to Him—and find His grace to be sufficient in my weakness.[12]

Jesus's pain on the cross was redemptive pain. His blood was redemptive blood. Isaiah 53:4–5 says:

> Surely he hath borne our griefs, and carried our sorrows: yet we did esteem him stricken, smitten of God, and afflicted. But he was wounded for our transgressions, he was bruised for our iniquities: the chastisement of our peace was upon him; and with his stripes we are healed.
>
> —Isaiah 53:4–5, kjv

Intimidation Factor

The enemy is intimidated by the potential on the inside of you. Your potential and purpose is seen more clearly by your enemy than by you. Your internal pain overshadows the greatness that God has assigned over your life. The greater the enemy's assault and attack on your life, the greater the assignment and plan that God has for you. When your thoughts take you back to a painful experience of your childhood, you may wonder, "Why did this happen to me? I was just a kid, vulnerable, young, and unable to defend myself. Why did I experience so much rejection and abuse? Why would fear haunt my heart at such an innocent age?"

In his book *Man's Search for Meaning*, Viktor E. Frankl says, "Those who have a 'why' to live, can bear with almost any 'how.'"[13] The pain of things that children encounter at an early age can be surmountable. These are the things that will affect your life in the years to come. Many of the issues and dysfunctional behaviors that adults are dealing with today stem from the pain of their childhood. By the time a high school diploma is placed in your hands, before you ever marry and have a family of your own, as you begin to search for your purpose and what you are going to do with your life, your insecurities and low self-worth attack your purpose and limit your capacity to dream. Your passions and aspirations slowly begin to dwindle. The hopes and dreams of your young adulthood become your nightmares.

You attempt to defy the voice of brokenness that has verbally assaulted your identity. Your answer to the haunting voice is to immerse yourself in efforts to achieve and gain accolades. It is your brokenness that drives you to find your identity and self-worth in your accomplishments and the approval of others. Your life becomes a constant audition for the next performance. You put on the appearance of a driven high achiever. What you cannot reveal is that your self-confidence and success is actually a cover-up for the insecurities that have become the addiction of your own fanfare. Your performance has become a sedative to your brokenness.

The enemy is not threatened by who you are but by who you will become. The answer to your questions about why you went through so much early in your life is not that the enemy was threatened by who you were. Your enemy was intimidated by who you were destined to become. Your potential had to be interrupted and halted. The enemy will not succeed; wholeness is coming to every broken place in your life. Your early introduction to pain and hurt has only made you more militant, only served to make you more relentless in discovering the answer as to why so much attention was given to your purpose. Your curiosity about the potential inside you is mounting. What put you on hell's radar before puberty? The world is waiting for your fingertips to touch a generation. One thing is certain: the world will know that you've been here.

BROKEN HOMES

The term broken home is used to define a family in which the parents have divorced. I understand the labeling and agree. However, the definition goes beyond a marriage that has ended in divorce. There are many other contributing factors that are worthy of consideration in a broken home situation. Every family has a level of brokenness. You might have been brought up in a single-parent home or with no parents; your home was provided by the state. You may have been raised in a blended family. You may have grown up in a Christian family with biological parents who sacrificed to provide the things that you needed to grow and become a healthy adult.

No matter what kind of family you grew up with, brokenness has a way of finding you. Its agenda is to assassinate your giftedness and God's purpose for your life. The silver spoon can quickly turn into the knife that is used to assault the promise of Jeremiah 29:11, God's plan to prosper you and give you hope and a future. Allowing the enemy to continue to provide condolences to the broken places of your life will only delay your arrival to the place of God's wholeness. Lick your wounds and release the roar on the inside of you.

As parents, you must refuse to succumb to the guilt that the enemy uses to assault your motherhood or fatherhood.

If the parents of Jesus could lose Him for three days (Luke 2:43–46), you're not going to get everything right either. We ask the Holy Spirit to help us, and we do the best we can with the cradle. You may feel like you've lost your son or daughter. Mary and Joseph found Jesus. You, too, will find your son or daughter as well. It's never too late for wholeness to come into your life, and it's never too late for wholeness to come into your relationships.

The prophetic Word of God says in Luke 12:53 that a sign that the end is near is when fathers will be against their sons, sons will be against their fathers, mothers will be against their daughters, and daughters will be against their mothers. We must guard our hearts from the divisiveness of the enemy. Recognize and refuse to give the divisive spirit of the enemy access to your family.

Intimidated by the Cradle

I grew up watching James Garner in *The Rockford Files* and must admit my fondness of the 2004 chick flick *The Notebook* in which he would star. What I did not know was that this successful actor dealt with challenges and brokenness. His father was a violent man and a heavy drinker. When James's father would come home after a night of drinking, he would demand that James, just six years old, sing to him or suffer the consequences and be beaten.[14]

The abuse of his father would pale in comparison to that of his stepmother. As punishment, she forced James to wear a dress in public and called him Louise. The attempts to destroy his identity and dreams would fail. He survived his childhood assaults, entered the world of show business, and went on to star in several television series. He also played leading roles in more than fifty theatrical films. By the end of his life, he had spent nearly sixty years on the stage in Broadway, behind the camera as a producer, and on the screen as an actor.[15]

Jim Carrey, a comedian actor, has starred in many films that have given me and my family a good laugh. However, growing up, things were not always that humorous for him. At sixteen, Carrey and his family were homeless, living in a van. He dropped out of school and began working to generate income to provide for his family. His early childhood struggles would not destroy his dream to perform and make people laugh.[16] Jim Carrey's current net worth is $150 million. He has several residences, including a home in Malibu that is valued at over $13 million, a long way from the van he shared with his family of six as a teenager.[17]

Why would Herod, a powerful king, be intimidated by a two-year-old? Why would he put the face of a two-year-old on wanted posters? Why would Herod issue the command for all male boys two and under to be killed (Matt. 2:16)? Herod knew that Jesus was no older than two. Herod was not threatened by a two-year-old. It was who Jesus would become that made him nervous. It was His purpose that threatened him. It was the potential on the inside of Him that Herod feared. It was the king in Jesus that made Herod fear for his position. What was in Jesus was a threat to his kingdom. Herod was intimidated by the cradle.

Moses was not a threat as an infant when he would be sent down the Nile River. What was the fear factor for mighty Pharaoh in killing all the male Hebrew babies (Exod. 1:22)? Why was he intimidated? It was because God would raise up a basket case that He would anoint and use, a man who would be His voice of deliverance to the nation of Israel. Pharaoh sought to wipe out the purpose and potential of Moses, but his attempt to destroy him early was unsuccessful. God would put Moses in the house of Pharaoh and raise him on his dollar. Then He would use Moses as the man who would strip Pharaoh of his power. Pharaoh was intimidated by the cradle.

Joseph was a seventeen-year-old teenager who was

battling hormones and acne. Why the intimidation? Why the rejection? Why the pit? Why the prison? It was his dream that was intimidating. It was his coat of colors that was intimidating. (See Genesis 37, 39.)

The attacks against you that came early in your life, the pain and the hurt that filled your young heart, the attack on your identity and your self-esteem—the rejection, the abandonment, and the traps were all well-baited to lure your vulnerabilities. It was the enemy recognizing the greatness on the inside of you. The assignment and purpose on your life intimidated the enemy. He had to try to stop you before you got started. Things happened to you that left you wondering, "Why did I go through that? Why did that happen to me?" You couldn't see "the why" because "the why" hadn't happened yet.

The why occurred because God put a coat on you. The why happened because God assigned you to change the world. The why transpired because you were destined to be God's voice to the nations.

If you can ever move past the whys and become the why, if you can push through the hurt, the enemy will regret he ever tried to stop you because his hindrance only made you stronger, more appreciative, and grateful for where you are and what God has done in your life. The Scriptures say that if Jesus's persecutors had known who He really was, they would have never crucified Him (1 Cor. 2:8). If they had known that His cross would become His crown, His stripes man's healing, His blood man's redemption, they never would have killed Him.

If the enemy had known that what he put you through would only make you tougher, he would have let you be. If he had realized that the trauma he caused in your life would push you to a deeper, more intimate relationship with Jesus, he would never have messed with you. If he had foreseen that the crushing of the olives in your life would only produce a stronger anointing, he would have left you alone. If he had guessed that the hurt would equip you and arm you with weapons to be used against him, he would have never interfered. Make the devil regret he ever messed with you. Don't get stuck in the whys but become the why.

> Pain insists upon being attended to. God whispers to us in our pleasures, speaks in our conscience, but shouts in our pains. It is His megaphone to rouse a deaf world.[18]
>
> —C. S. LEWIS

PAIN MAY SAVE YOUR LIFE

Physical pain is a signal that is sent to the brain when there has been an injury to the body. It is a message that you need to give attention to the area from where the pain is coming. Pain is simply the body's warning signal or, as C. S. Lewis said, it is God's megaphone.

Several years ago I was experiencing intense pain in my abdomen. I went to my doctor, and the first question he asked me was, "Where does it hurt? Where is the pain coming from?" The pain was used to diagnose my situation. I was immediately sent to the hospital to be prepared for surgery. My appendix was at risk of bursting, which would have sent infection throughout my body. It was the megaphone of pain that would save my life. It refused to allow me to ignore what was broken and damaged on the inside of me. The pain was relentless because it would not rest until the broken was made whole. It wasn't long after surgery that I was up and about my business. The pain was gone after it served its purpose.

The pain that comes from the trauma and broken places of your life is God's megaphone that reveals where you are broken. The emotional and psychological pain that you are experiencing serves to diagnose what you are feeling and demands an explanation for behaviors. In essence, the pain you're feeling right now may save your life. Pain is given no gratitude and has never received a thank you card. However, there are few things that have served you better.

The Cry

When I was diagnosed with appendicitis, there was a certain area that the doctor pushed that triggered a reaction which indicated what was broken had been located. As uncomfortable as it can be at times, learn to trust your pain. Pain may be your closest ally. Pain may save your life. Trust your pain and observe your response to the places when pushed that trigger a reaction.

As a father, as much as you would like to take away the pain of your children, you have to trust the pain. It is through pain that kids are able to communicate that they are hurting. A baby cannot talk, but there is a cry that alerts parents when there is a serious problem. A mother and father can recognize the different cries that come from their baby. They cry when they're hungry, wet, uncomfortable, or mad. But there is a special cry that comes from a baby that tears your heart out, a cry that lets you know they are hurting. This cry urges you to rush to their side and causes you to cradle your child in your arms. As much as you want to take the pain from your child, you cannot because it serves a purpose.

There is a sound, a cry that comes from God's sons and daughters, a cry that brings God to your side. This cry causes Him to cradle you in His arms. God wants the pain and suffering to be over, but it must serve its purpose. God receives no pleasure from your pain. Your heavenly Father finds it more difficult watching you suffer than you do watching your own children suffer. God is with us; He never leaves us, never forsakes us. He has a soft spot for those who are broken and hurting. When our pain is the greatest, His presence is the strongest.

The LORD is close to the brokenhearted and saves those who are crushed in spirit.

—PSALM 34:18

CHAPTER 3

TEAR DOWN THESE WALLS

TEAR DOWN THIS wall! "General Secretary Gorbachev, if you seek peace, if you seek prosperity for the Soviet Union and Eastern Europe...tear down this wall!"[1] These are the historic words that were spoken by American President Ronald Reagan in his speech on June 12, 1987. President Reagan was addressing the people of West Berlin just feet away from the Berlin Wall. His audience was not just the people of West Berlin; his address was heard by the world. It was one of those moments in history when Americans were proud of their leader. As he stood tall and strong with conviction and passion, President Reagan declared these words that are forever etched in history: "Mr. Gorbachev, tear down this wall!" The wall that President Reagan spoke of was the Berlin Wall, a wall that was built in 1961 by the Communists to keep Germans from fleeing Communist-controlled East Berlin. On November 9, 1989, two years after President Reagan made his historical speech, the walls would come down.[2]

STICKS AND STONES AND TONGUES

There are events that happen in life that are very traumatic. Trauma causes not only physical pain but also deep emotional pain. "Sticks and stones may break my bones but names will never hurt me" is a phrase that first appeared

25

in the mid to late 1800s. The earliest appearance I found was in the *Christian Recorder* of March 1862, a publication of the African Methodist Episcopal Church.[3] I understand the phrase and its intended purpose and have to admit that I borrowed from it at times in adolescence to ward off schoolyard bullies.

Even as an adolescent, you didn't trust your defense. At night with your head on your pillow, your thoughts would revisit the cruel words of your bully. It would have been easier to take one to the chin and certainly quicker to recover. Broken bones heal much quicker than a broken heart. Sticks and stones break bones, but tongues damage self-esteem and self-worth. When you recall the physical pain from sticks and stones, you don't feel the pain of the injury; but when you remember the words and traumatic experiences in your life, there is substantial emotional pain.

Physical pain can be used as a distraction from the emotional pain in your life. But emotional pain is never a distraction from your physical pain. Those who cut themselves do so as a distraction from the deep emotional pain on the inside of them. Though distracted, the brokenness does not go away. The message to the emotionally wounded is that your pain and hurt is real. You need to know that Jesus was wounded so you don't have to be, that there is healing and wholeness that can come to every broken place in your life. Jesus understands your pain. He feels your pain. He loves you more than your hurt says you deserve. You feel so broken and useless, but Jesus says, "I love you and believe in you. Call out to Me and let Me wrap My arms around you and heal every hurt and broken place in your life."

The truth is that sticks and stones do hurt and so do tongues! Notably, when you begin to believe them or they come from the tongue of one you trust, words cut deeper than stones, break hearts, and shatter souls. Of the 500,000 words in the English vocabulary, your traducer knows the exact choice of words to cause you to run for the wall.

INVISIBLE WALLS

Walls become the fortress of the broken—walls that may or may not have been erected intentionally or were even known to exist. They may not be visible, but don't be mistaken about their existence. The strength of their intended purpose is very much at work in the lives of the broken.

It did not take long after the Berlin Wall was expunged from the city that it was no longer visible. Soon after, its facts were nestled safely in the history books. The dust was clearing from the remnants of the cursed. The last of the political speeches had been spoken. It would be ascertained from the East and the West that a wall still existed. It was an invisible wall but a wall nonetheless. The 1989 removal of the Berlin Wall gave passage to all who had been restricted. The invisible wall would not be as forgiving. While the Communists were building a wall to oppress and hurt the commonality, the people were building invisible walls—walls that entrapped the emotional pain and hurt that had accumulated for over twenty-eight years. It would be discovered that it was not only the Berlin Wall that had taken away the freedom of man. That would be too much power to give to reinforced concrete. What would be most difficult to demolish were the invisible walls that had been constructed in the hearts of the emotionally broken.

What serves as the greatest obstacle in your journey from brokenness to wholeness is the invisible wall you put up that becomes your prison. Many come and stand at your invisible wall and, like President Reagan, plead for you to tear it down. Your wife stands at the wall of your heart and shouts, "Tear down these walls!" You've built walls to protect yourself from the enemies of fear and insecurity. You've built walls that allow sex but no intimacy. You've built walls that won't let her in and won't let you out, walls that won't let you talk. Her heart yearns for what she needs to hear that you cannot say. What you have learned to live without leaves her empty and alone.

Your husband stands at the wall of your heart and screams, "Tear down these walls!" You've built walls as security from the places of rejection in your life. You've built walls that keep you from releasing the treasure on the inside of you, walls that falsely recognize new relationships as a possibility for rejection. You sneak out from behind your wall wearing a mask only to be met by the exhausting expectations of acceptance. You've built walls that are so thick that you can't hear the voice of love and approval that comes from your husband just on the other side. Your invisible walls will not let him in. Your walls have become your boundaries to protect yourself from rejection. The innocent suffer and so do you because there is no intimacy for those who choose to live behind invisible walls.

Your dream and destiny stand at the wall of your purpose and wail, "Tear down these walls!" You've erected walls to protect yourself from the failures of your past. You've built walls to protect yourself from every fumble in your life, every missed and failed opportunity. You've constructed walls to protect yourself from your haters, those who were either too shallow or too intimidated to see the embryonic destiny on the inside of you. Your purpose stands at the wall to elicit the vast greatness that dwells within you. It shouts with the same conviction and passion of President Reagan: "Tear down this wall!"[4]

> The task of leadership is not to put greatness into humanity, but to elicit it, for the greatness is already there.[5]
>
> —JOHN BUCHAN

ALABASTER JAR

In the Gospel of Mark there is the story of Mary, a woman who comes to Jesus. She brings with her an alabaster jar of expensive perfume. In a room full of people, her next move grabs the attention of the skeptics. With intention, she breaks open the jar to release the fragrance within, a sacrificial act that touches the heart of Jesus. It moved Him so deeply that He would speak of it in the fourteenth chapter of Mark:

> While he was in Bethany, reclining at the table in the home of Simon the Leper, a woman came with an alabaster jar of very expensive perfume, made of pure nard. She broke the jar and poured the perfume on his head. Some of those present were saying indignantly to one another, "Why this waste of perfume? It could have been sold for more than a year's wages and the money given to the poor." And they rebuked her harshly. "Leave her alone," said Jesus. "Why are you bothering her? She has done a beautiful thing to me....Truly I tell you, wherever the gospel is preached throughout the world, what she has done will also be told, in memory of her."
>
> —MARK 14:3–6, 9

The alabaster jar had to be broken to release the fragrance inside. The perfume was not wasted when the jar was broken to release it. The perfume would have been wasted if it had remained locked within the jar. The fragrance left in the jar was of no benefit. The fragrance of your gift and purpose is of no benefit to anyone behind walls. The tearing down of your walls is equivalent to Mary breaking open her alabaster jar. Tearing down your walls allows the vast greatness in you to be released upon those to whom you have been assigned.

The world has not yet seen all that you are gifted to do.

They have yet to smell the fragrance of your full potential. As the walls are torn down in your life to allow healing and wholeness to come to the places you have hidden and protected, the scent of God's anointing will be left on you to touch a generation. Jesus mentions in verse 9 that Mary's act of breaking the alabaster jar and releasing the fragrance within will be told wherever the gospel is preached. When your walls come down to release your dreams and giftedness that have been confined, this is the worship that flows from your life that honors and pleases the Lord.

WALL OF SHAME

The wall of shame was scrupulously labeled by Mayor Willy Brandt of West Berlin.[6] The wall became a concrete expression of a prison for those whom it contained. It was a wall that would divide families and neighbors, a wall of shame that would divide a city and a nation. The shame of the wall was that it restricted entrance and passage out.

You have put up walls to hide your brokenness and pain. Your wall is one of shame because you built it to protect yourself, but it also locks you in. Your wall becomes a self-made prison. You didn't intend for it to be a prison. The wall went up as a safe house for your pain and brokenness, a haven for silent suffering. The wall has become the residence of your broken dreams and hopes. It has become your city of refuge. It is the place you run to when life threatens you with anything that resembles or exposes what has caused great pain in your life. Your wall is a prison that you warden and manage, a prison in which you established the rules and boundaries, a prison where you do not permit conjugal visits. Intimacy is too vulnerable and threatens the fortified walls that you have erected.

The ignominy of the walls that you have erected in your life is that you are never brought to a place of healing and wholeness. You sentenced yourself to life imprisonment behind the walls that you built. Instead of allowing your heart to be healed and made whole from the abuse and assaults it has taken, you create a wall of shame—layers of callousness that leave you with a hard, desensitized heart. A heart that has been desensitized does not have the luxury of choosing when, where, or with whom to be sensitive.

In Ephesians 4, the Apostle Paul says that when the heart has been hardened, it loses all sensitivity (vv. 18–19). It is dangerous to have a heart that cannot feel. You not only become insensitive to the pain of others but insensitive to your own pain. You not only fail to convey love but lose the necessary sensitivity to receive love. The most jeopardous concern about a heart that is walled beneath callousness and hardness is that it becomes desensitized to the Holy Spirit. You lose the ability to follow His leadership for your life. You can no longer respond to His correction through His gentle nudging. You become dull to the sense of right and wrong.

The Apostle Paul warns of such a condition when he speaks about the conscience being seared with a hot iron in 1 Timothy 4:2. Paul is talking about a heart that becomes cauterized and rendered insensitive. Paul states that one of the indicators of the last days is when hearts will be seared with a hot iron.

WALLS OF A CALLOUS HEART

When we think of those with hard hearts, we think of men and women who commit violent acts with little or no remorse. We think of the biblical example of Pharaoh whose heart was hardened. We think of Ananias and Sapphira, who lied to the Holy Spirit. We may even think of the men who ordered the building of the Berlin Wall that brought oppression and brokenness to a nation and thousands of families. These would each be good examples of individuals with hearts that had grown hard and callous.

What we overlook and find hard to believe is that there

are those of you who consider yourself a good person. You have integrity and character. You try to live right and do well by others. You have careers and families. You are church attendees and honor God with your tithe. How could my heart that has always known compassion and tenderness ever become hard and callous? How could my heart that has been sensitive to the Holy Spirit and to the needs of my family and others become impenetrable? You make imbecilic statements such as, "I know that can happen to others but definitely not to me."

No one is exempt from being a candidate of a hard and callous heart. When we don't correctly deal with the hurts and pains that we accrue, when we recoil from the struggles and trauma that come into our lives, when we don't confront the brokenness and allow the Holy Spirit to bring us to the place of healing and wholeness, there are walls of callousness that wrap around our hearts that create a hardness. The heart grows cold and callous. The process is progressive until the day of self-awareness comes, and you ask yourself the hard question: "How did I get to this place?" You arrived by abiding in a place where your heart was AWOL, in a marriage in which your heart checked out, in a ministry that your heart was no longer in. Worship flowed from your mouth, but it was a stench in the nostrils of God because it was heartless and void of passion.

In Ephesians 4:18, the Apostle Paul says they were darkened in their understanding and separated from the life of God because of the ignorance that was in them due to the hardening of their hearts. Don't allow your obedience to deceive you into thinking your heart is well. You can continue in obedience without a pure heart. People stay because it is the right thing to do, but their heart is not in it. It is a matter of time before the heart and the will to obey become exhausted pulling in opposite directions.

WARNINGS OF A HEART ATTACK

The human heart is made up of muscular tissue. Its function is to keep your blood circulating through the arteries, veins, and capillaries of your body. In 2014 the life expectancy of a man in the US was seventy-six years;[7] the heart will beat over 3 billion times.[8] You rely on a strong and healthy heart for your survival. The physical heart will send out warnings when it is under attack. Adhering to these warning signs could very well save your life.

The heart that I have spoken of throughout this chapter is what the Jewish people believed to be the seat of emotions. In Luke 19:41, Jesus wept over the city. He was moved with compassion. In Matthew 20:34, Jesus touched the blinded eyes of two beggars. He was moved with compassion. In Matthew 9:36, Jesus saw those who were helpless and without a shepherd. He was moved with compassion. The Greek word used here for "moved with compassion" means moved from the bowels or the inward parts.[9] The Jews believed the bowels of the heart were the seat of emotions. Jesus felt and was moved with compassion from deep within His heart.

I'm speaking of a heart that can make the face cheerful and a heart, when aching, that can crush the spirit (Prov. 15:13). I'm referring to a heart that plans your course and allows the Lord to determine your steps (16:9). I am talking about what the prophet Samuel was looking for when he arrived at the house of Jesse to anoint the next king. In 1 Samuel 16:7, the Lord tells Samuel that people look at the outward appearance, but God looks at the heart—the part of you that Jesus was referring to when He revealed the greatest commandment was your heart: "Love the Lord your God with all your heart" (Matt. 22:37).

Recognizing the signs that the organ in your body about the size of a fist is under attack may save your life. Noticing the signs that your heart, which sits at the seat of all that you are, is in danger of becoming hard and callous may very well save not only your life but your dream and purpose. Giving attention to these threatening signs may save your marriage and other meaningful relationships.

In order for you to recognize the signs that your heart is under attack, you must be familiar with them. One sign is that there is no celebration or pleasure from the things in your life that in the past would have caused you to break out in a silly victory dance. You are losing your ability to see the wins. Another sign is when you find it difficult to cry and show emotion. Remember, if God did not intend for us to cry, He wouldn't have made us with tear ducts. Something else that should be a warning flag is when it gets difficult to see the good in people and situations. You begin to live your life like the grandfather who woke up with Limburger cheese in his mustache that had been placed there by his grandson without his knowing. The old man walked into the living room and said, "It stinks in here." He then shuffled into the kitchen and said, "It stinks in here." He moved outside onto the front porch and declared, "The whole world stinks!" If your whole world is giving off an odor, it may be coming from your own heart. Another sign that your heart is under attack is when things that you used to be passionate about have departed and left nothing in their place.

When the heart becomes hard and callous, you lose passion. There were places in your life that you once were so passionate about, but no longer; for passion cannot burn in a heart that has become rocky with stones that have slowly mounted into a wall. Passion refuses to reside behind this wall. Passion will not be your cell mate in this prison with no place to manifest. Without passion, your life becomes mundane and begins to introduce you to the dark place of depression. Depression is the dungeon of the prison—the darker, deeper place behind the wall. It is a place where hope, one of the last residents of your heart, is brought to arbitration. In Jeremiah 17:9, the prophet Jeremiah warns of the double-dealings of the heart. A heart that once had such great residents as hope and passion now welcomes bitterness and hatred to the neighborhood, contributors of additional layers of callousness to a heart that has already become hard.

HEALING OF A BROKEN HEART

The prayer of King David speaks of the importance of a heart that is healthy and whole. After experiencing failure and brokenness in his life, King David, with everything that he stood to lose, did not ask God for his kingdom and palace. David never mentions his crown. He does not ask God to be spared from embarrassment with the people he is called to lead. The gold, cattle, and property are not what the king is fearful of losing. We hear the heart of a king who is crying out for wholeness. His heart had become hard and callous. David had once relied on his heart to be tender to the voice and whispers of his God; but in this situation, God had to call on one of His choice servants by the name of Nathan to confront the king. This confrontation would draw equal attention to David's sin with Bathsheba and the fact that David's heart had become cold and callous.

In Psalm 51, we hear the cry of a king for the healing and wholeness of his heart. David was broken over his brokenness. His cry was one of humility and fear of a life without passion and sensitivity to the presence of the God he loved. He prayed, "God it's not about the throne. It's not about the crown. It's not about the gold and land. It's not about my title and reputation. I lay all of that down. God, all that I ask is that You please create in me a clean heart and take not Your Holy Spirit from me. Unwrap the callousness of my heart. Lead me out from behind the walls that I've built. Take away this stony, stubborn heart and give me a tender, responsive heart." (See Psalm 51:1–17 and Ezekiel 11:19.)

Tor Auf

On November 9, 1989, there would be chants from both sides of the Berlin Wall, shouts from both genders. Each generation could be heard with loud, vigorous cries of "Tor auf!" Their unified declaration was "Tor auf," German for "open the gate."[10] For some, the cry meant "Open the gate, and let me out!" For others, it meant "Open the gate, and let me in!" As the bulldozers and cranes began to tear down the walls, it was as if the sound of the breaking of chains and shackles could be heard. The instrument that confined a nation and a people like a prison was torn to the ground.

The heavy equipment operators in the demolition of the wall that had oppressed the people of Berlin for over twenty-eight years would be assisted by those who would come to be labeled the wall "woodpeckers."[11] With hammers and chisels, these wall woodpeckers would take part in their own healing and wholeness. They would tirelessly chip away at the wall that had imprisoned them. With a hammer in one hand and a chisel in the other, the shout of "Tor auf" could be heard as they would come out from behind the wall that had taken so much from them.

Tearing of the Veil

From the cross Jesus would shout, "It is finished!" (John 19:30, NKJV). With more power and authority than President Reagan, Jesus would bellow, "Tear down these walls!" The voice of the omnipotent God would command the veil to be torn, a wall that was sixty feet long, thirty feet wide, and four inches thick.[12] The great theologian Josephus said that horses tied to each side of the veil could not pull it apart.[13] The veil was so massive it would take three hundred priests to attend to it.[14] This veil was a wall of shame because it barred all but the high priest from the presence of God. It walled out man from God their Creator.

Behind the veil was the holy place. It was here that the ark of the covenant would reside along with the mercy seat, symbols of God's divine presence, mercy, and forgiveness. Once a year the high priest would carefully and reverently enter behind the veil. He would sprinkle the blood of a sacrificial animal upon the mercy seat, a blood sacrifice for the sin of the people and nation.

The veil being torn was God's message to you that there will never be a wall that will separate you from His presence. Bring your brokenness, bring your hurt and pain, bring your heart that is callous and hard. The message of the torn veil is bring your sin, your failures, your shame and dysfunction. Jesus is saying, "I am your great High Priest. I am your mercy seat."

Jesus shouted from the cross, "It is finished!" His shout was so loud the veil began to tear from the top to the bottom. The earth shook, and rocks began to crumble. The tombs of the dead burst open, bringing the dead to life (Matt. 27:51–53).

> Some people die at 25 and aren't buried until they're 75.[15]
>
> —BENJAMIN FRANKLIN

When you break out from behind your walls, the dead things in your life will begin to live. Your dream and vision will develop a pulse. Your marriage and relationships will experience a resurrection. There is going to be an awakening in your life of newfound passions and expectations.

The power that tore the veil that separated man from God is the same power that can tear down the walls in your life and bring healing and wholeness to a heart that has grown callous and hard.

CHAPTER 4

REINFORCED WALLS

THE ENORMOUS BERLIN Wall extended twenty-eight miles through Berlin, a concrete curtain of oppression. This wall reinforced the views and ideology of the powers of that day. The gargantuan wall towered over the people whom it was assigned to oppress. It stood twelve feet tall and four feet thick and was bolstered with thousands of pounds of concrete and steel, reinforced with electricity and barbed wire, and capped with an enormous pipe that made penetrating the wall nearly impossible. Waiting on the east side of the wall was more reinforcement to assure that its purpose would not be defied. Pits of soft sand lined the wall to track the footprints of anyone who, by chance, was able to scale it. These pits were hallmarked the "Death Strip." There were floodlights, bloodthirsty dogs, trip-wire machine guns, and soldiers who guarded with orders to shoot on sight.[1] These reinforcements contributed to make the wall stronger and sent a message that to escape was beyond the bounds of possibility. The idea of the reinforcement was that any hope of freedom and escape was nothing more than a pipe dream.

PIPE DREAM

Those who have been sentenced behind the walls of Souza-Baranowski Correctional Center in Massachusetts have but a pipe dream to escape. SBCC is one of the most secure prisons in the world, a prison reinforced with six hundred guards and monitored by the omnipotent eye of a robotic overlord. Forty-two graphic interfaced computer terminals drive a keyless system that controls everything from the doors to the water to the PA system and the vehicle gates. The premises of the prison are recorded 24 hours a day with 370 high-definition cameras. The institution is reinforced by the highest strength concrete and steel available.[2] The reinforcements have created a pipe dream for those whom the prison confines. SBCC is a prison of false hope from which none have escaped.

Consider the emotional trauma in your life, the hurt and the pain that have been sheltered by your walls. Evaluate the iron curtain of what has ruptured in you—brokenness that has yet to make the journey to healing and wholeness, infelicity that has led to the construction of walls that have become your prison—walls with a pipe dream of amnesty. Of the despairing stories behind prison walls, perhaps the most saddening are those of hearts that once were full of optimism and reverie but now have been abducted by a pipe dream, an unrealistic hope of freedom that continues to build reinforcements for imprisonment. Your wall that formed from the broken places in your life furnishes the reinforcements that are needed to ensure a life of confinement.

TENDER HEART

As I was driving to the office one day, I heard the Holy Spirit speaking to my heart. The words that He spoke would garner the attention of my convictions. He would say only two words and then would leave me to sort through my emotions, in search of insight for the purpose behind this heavenly visitation. The gentle divine utterance was "tender heart." This one statement had me calling for a spiritual EKG. The results would bring a self-awareness of the fact that those who hold titles, positions, or clergy credentials are not exempt from a heart that has lost its tenderness. This phrase would serve as a reminder that the God who has enlisted me into His service is more concerned with what He is doing in me than what He is doing through me, that what is done in His name is not intended to desensitize the tenderness of the heart.

With his pen of wisdom, Solomon wrote in Proverbs 4:23: "Above all else, guard your heart, for everything you do flows from it." Guard your heart from what is contributing to its loss of tenderness. Your heart is the spring that supplies all that you need to fulfill your dream and destiny. Guard it well and keep it tender. We are commanded in 1 Peter 3:8 to be tenderhearted (ESV). God wants our hearts to be tender. He desires for His children to have hearts that are tender toward the Holy Spirit because a heart that is tender can hear His voice. A tender heart can be counseled and instructed. A tender heart that knows empathy can be compassionate and love what God loves.

In life you have been through things that have caused you great pain, trauma that has caused severe mental and emotional pain in your heart. Maybe you've experienced anguish from the mistreatment and rejection of an unpleasant divorce, a divorce that dragged your children through custody battles which only added to the agony. You've accumulated brokenness that has never been healed and made whole. Your heart has been abnormal for so long it has become your new normal. The matter of contention is that the heart has lost its tenderness.

COUNTERREFORMATION

In Romans 12:2, the Apostle Paul offers great wisdom. He says not to be conformed to the things of this world. The first part of the word *conformed* is *con* as in convict. You have imprisoned everything in your life that has brought you pain and brokenness. You incarcerated in your heart the verbal abuse that assaulted your self-worth and enclosed the pain that accrued when you were given up for adoption. You have asked yourself a thousand times, "Why did my parents not want me?" The longer you continue to give rejection and abandonment an address in your heart, the more your heart will lose its tenderness. You have incarcerated the things that have caused your brokenness and insecurity. You have given betrayal and broken trust a residence in your heart. This only reinforces the walls that circumscribe your heart and shave away its tenderness.

The Apostle Paul says not to conform to the things of this world. The brokenness that you have incarcerated will attempt to reform you and counter the Designer's original blueprint of what you were created to be. You have been fearfully and wonderfully created by God (Ps. 139:14), made in such a way that can never be duplicated. It is flattering to be imitated, but you can never be duplicated because you are the Designer's original copy. What you have grown to hate about yourself is the counterreformation of your brokenness, attitudes, and disposition that has vacuumed up the greatness and potential of your Designer and His plan and destiny for your life.

POVERTY SPIRIT

The emotional brokenness in your life has taken your self-worth on a counterreformation that has created a feeling of inadequacy and a poverty mentality, a mind-set that says you don't deserve better. You remain in an abusive relationship because the poverty mentality says you don't deserve better. You create a pattern of being involved in one abusive relationship after another. A poverty mentality attacks your attitudes and expectations. It's not that you struggle; you expect to struggle. It's not that you lack; you expect to lack. It's not that you fail; you expect to fail. In fact, you plan for failure.

> Whether you think you can, or you think you cannot, you're right.[3]
>
> —HENRY FORD

Poverty happens in you before it happens around you. You had a poverty mentality before your bank account went in the red. Having money does not defeat a poverty mentality. There are many who have come into money either through an inheritance or the right numbers on a lottery ticket only to become bankrupt a few years later. A poverty mentality deceives you into thinking that the solution to your problem is external. Your focus is on what you don't have instead of what you do have. Discover the vast greatness of the Designer's original plan that He carefully placed within you.

You may have been around poverty, but don't let it get in you. Several years ago, I was preaching a service in New York. I noticed a Hispanic young man who was sobbing uncontrollably. I approached him and asked him his name. He told me his name and stated that he was sixteen years old. After talking with him for a few moments, it became evident to me that this young teenager had a hunger and passion for Jesus. There was an epic battle of the Designer's original plan and the counterreformation that was taking place in this young man's life.

During our conversation, we discussed what had brought out so much emotion in his visit to the altar. He asked me to pray with him for God to break the spirit of poverty off of his life. I have to admit that I was impressed with his request considering the hundreds of teenagers I had prayed with over the years who had shared with me more breakup stories than Dr. Phil and Oprah combined. The sincerity and maturity of his request left a lasting impression on my heart. He shared with me that though he came from a good family, he was brought up in a spirit of poverty. He mentioned that it became generational because his grandparents had the poverty spirit upon their life and family as well. I will never forget the prayer request that came from this sobbing sixteen-year-old teenager at the altar in New York, the financial capital of the world: "Pastor Johnny, please pray that God would break off of my life the spirit of poverty."

STINKING THINKING

The Apostle Paul says not to be conformed to this world. We also should not allow what we have been through to conform us. The great apostle continues to write and says, "But be transformed by the renewing of your mind" (Rom. 12:2). The first part of the word *transformed* is *trans*, as in transportation. In lieu of incarcerating your brokenness and giving it an address in your heart, transport it out of your heart by the renewing of your mind. Serve an eviction notice to the issues that have reinforced your brokenness and have affected the tenderness of your heart.

There may be changes that have come to many areas of your life, changes in behavior that have warranted the approval and applause of others, changes in the places you go and the language you use. You have found that the greatest battle and most difficult place to gain dominion are both in your mind. To rid yourself of stinking thinking is the most difficult task. Paul knew that it was going to take more than behavior modification to break away from the counterreformation that occurred from the brokenness and trauma in your life and return to the Designer's original plan. Paul connects the transformation in our life to the process of the renewing of our mind.

We witness the work of the Holy Spirit in this process in the writings of Ezekiel:

> A new heart also will I give you, and a new spirit will I put within you: and I will take the stony heart out of your flesh, and I will give you a heart of flesh.
>
> —EZEKIEL 36:26, KJV

Ezekiel is saying the Holy Spirit will take the heart that has gone through a counterreformation, bring it back to the Designer's original plan, and restore its tenderness. The Holy Spirit brings the heart back to Jesus. Both will assist you in the transformation through the renewing of your mind.

Many are dismayed to find that their old ways of thinking haven't changed even after surrendering their life to Jesus, after coming into a relationship with Him, after having their heart, which has been numb for years, suddenly overwhelmed by His saturating love, only to discover that stinking thinking is still present. The renewing of the mind is a process in which you take the lead. God decides who wins the war, but you determine who wins the battle.

You decide what you feed and what you starve. You starve out the oppression, bitterness, fear, and doubt, but you feed your mind His Word. You meditate on His Word. Every negative thought that surfaces in your mind should be answered with the truth of the Word of God. You expose your mind to His presence through prayer and worship. You die daily to self. Daily renew your mind by ushering it through the filter of the Holy Spirit. Paul said to bring every thought into the captivity of Christ (2 Cor. 10:5, KJV). Each day, each week, you begin to notice the old data and stinking thinking being deleted with every fresh download of the Word of God.

> And we all, who with unveiled faces contemplate the Lord's glory, are being transformed into his image with ever-increasing glory, which comes from the Lord, who is the Spirit.
>
> —2 CORINTHIANS 3:18

Remember it is a walk with God. There may be days you feel like you went the wrong way, had a wrong attitude, or made a wrong decision. Your wall has discovered that your failures serve well as reinforcement. They have proven so many times in your life to send you running for the wall. Champions learn to use failure as valuable training instead of a reason to quit the game. Stay in the game!

WRONG WAY RIEGELS

Your walls will go on a quest for support, hunting for reinforcement that is equal to the intimidation of bloodthirsty dogs and machine gun trip wires. This reinforcement acts as the "death strip" of your life where your footprints of failure are visible. The instant you think you are obtaining the dauntlessness to advance beyond your concrete bubble, your death strip shows you the footprints of your past. These prints cause you to race for your wall. They represent the places in your life where there has been failure and shame. The highlight reels and footage of every fumble and blocked shot in your life. Your history can be used as reinforcement to your confinement.

New Year's Day 1929 will forever be a footprint in the sand for Wrong Way Riegels, a name that Roy Riegels would carry for the rest of his collegiate football career and beyond.[4] It was the Rose Bowl, nicknamed "The Granddaddy of Them All." The oldest of the bowl games, the Rose Bowl was first played in 1902.[5] It was a capacity crowd of 70,000 screaming fans who had packed into the stadium. They had come to watch undefeated Georgia Tech and their once-beaten opponent University of California in the nation's only bowl game. It was the biggest game of the season, a game that these young athletes had dreamed of since Pop Warner and sandlot neighborhood football. It would be in the second quarter that Roy Riegels, the center and captain of the Golden Bears, would experience fifteen minutes that would leave his prints in the death strip of sand. It would be a perpetual reminder of his haunting failure. The game was scoreless with both teams dispensing everything they had.[6]

Then it happened; the ball broke loose from Georgia Tech's John Thomason who was nicknamed "Stumpy," a nickname that "Wrong Way" Roy would have gladly swapped to escape the reminder of that calamitous fifteen minutes. Roy, alerted that the ball was on the ground, picked it up and ran sixty-nine yards in the wrong direction. This sixty-nine-yard sprint would place upon him a label that would not dodder. It was the biggest game of his college career, and he ran the wrong way. If it was not for the speedy Benny Lom, the quarterback of the Golden Bears, chasing Roy and screaming frantically after him, Riegels would not have slowed down enough for the host of Yellow Jacket tacklers to emerge upon him, bringing him to the ground at the one-yard line, only inches away from the end zone of Georgia Tech.[7]

The death strip of Roy Riegels would boast prints of 4,500 newspaper stories, an estimated 250,000 column inches written about this one mistake.[8] This reinforcement of the memory of his failure had already begun to be etched in his wall. At halftime, Roy, the captain of the Golden Bears, would take off his jersey and pads in total humiliation, removing himself from the game. Coach Nibs Price, the head coach and leader of the team, would have to move quickly before his captain retreated further behind the wall that was already summoning his star athlete.[9]

Roy said, "Coach, I can't do it...I've ruined you. I've ruined my school. I've ruined myself. I couldn't face the crowd in that stadium to save my life."[10] The reinforcements collaborated to keep Roy behind the walls of the locker room and out of the game. Coach Price would look at the brokenness of Roy Riegels as the bloodthirsty dogs and machine gun trip wires began to position themselves as reinforcements of the wall of "Wrong Way" Roy. Coach Price would break the silence with words not only for Roy but for every person who has ever failed, every person who has ever ran the wrong way. His words are for those who have allowed a failure to reinforce their confinement behind the wall of their prison. As the words of President Reagan are forever etched in history, the words of Coach Nibs Price will never be forgotten: "Roy, get up and get back. The game is only half over."[11]

Roy would rejoin his teammates and play a stellar second half. Roy Riegels finished out his college career and in 1991 was inducted into the Rose Bowl Hall of Fame.[12]

Resist the reinforcement of your failures which are purposed to keep you out of the game. Come out from behind your wall and get back in the game. The second half is going to be your best half. The second half is where you make your mark. The second half is where you imprint on your generation.

SECOND HALF

You have been through ordeals that have caused you pain, brokenness, and trauma that sent you into survival mode. Thoughts of rising from the ashes are quickly dismissed by the imagery of what caused such damage and brokenness in your life. Comeback stories are good for motivational speakers, but they're for the other team. You have allowed what has brought brokenness into your life to torment and beat you up for so long. You are in danger of losing one of God's greatest and most overlooked gifts, the gift of hope. Hope is the gift that often abides in childlike faith. It has yet to meet the repetitive brunt of the invader of dreams and purpose that relentlessly pursues to embezzle from the heart all that God has gifted, including the treasured gift of hope.

A father was running late to his son's little league game. After finally arriving, he noticed that the score was 18 to 0 in favor of the other team. As he was speaking with his son, he said, "I am so sorry." The little boy looked up at his dad and said, "It's all right, Dad. We haven't been up to bat yet." That is hope, and that is the gift that you want to protect that God has put in your heart. No matter how your situation appears, no matter the score, you need to have hope.

Like Roy Riegels, you ran the wrong way. In embarrassment, you have headed for the locker room with full intention of never returning. Don't miss the second half. Get back in the game. Champions are born in the second half. Champions emerge in the second half. Walt Disney was fired by a news editor who said he lacked creativity. His dream was rejected 302 times for financing.[13] The second half? Well, you can go to Orlando or Anaheim and see the end result for yourself. Stephen King had his first book rejected thirty times. He became so frustrated that he quit and threw it in the trash. His wife dug his dream out of the garbage, and he resubmitted the book one more time. In the second half, Stephen King has sold more than 350 million copies of his books.[14] Some of the greatest songs, books, and creative ideas the world has never seen have been trashed. What do you need to dig out of the trash?

Billy Graham preached one of his first sermons to forty people. He had four sermons in his repertoire at the time and he preached all four in eight minutes with his knees knocking and sweat dripping from his fingertips. "After the service was over with, one of the men of the church came up to Billy and told him, 'Boy you better go back to school and get a lot more education because you're not gonna make it.'"[15] The man would be proven to be wrong, and in the second half Billy Graham has preached the gospel of Christ in person to more than 200 million people. Add to that the countless millions more over the airwaves and in films, it is estimated he has shared his message with over 2 billion people, the most of anyone in history.[16] Nearly 3 million have responded to the invitation he offers at the end of his sermons.[17] When America needs a chaplain or pastor to help inaugurate or bury a president or to bring comfort in times of terrible tragedy, it turns, more often than not, to Billy Graham.[18]

He has appeared on Gallup's list of the most admired people fifty-five times, more than anyone else in the world.[19] Let these stories remind you that your failure is not final. Get back in the game. There is a second half to be played.

NEVER SAY DIE

I will never be able to forget when Coach Tony Dungy was fired by the Tampa Bay Buccaneers.[20] He had captured the hearts of the Tampa Bay Area, my family included. Coach Dungy is greatly missed, not only for his outstanding leadership and knowledge of the game but for his character and gentleman-like attitude with which he conducted himself on and off the field.

It was raining the night Coach Dungy packed up his office for his move to Indianapolis for his next coaching assignment. There he would win a Super Bowl on February 7, 2007.[21] As we were watching the big game from our home on our flat screen TV, we could hear the shouts and cheers throughout our neighborhood joined with thousands of others throughout the area who were cheering for the Colts—not out of disloyalty for Tampa but out of love for the coach. On the rainy night Dungy packed up his office with the Bucs, I would lose one of my Sunday-afternoon-football-watching buddies—my wife. As the news covered the story, we watched as Coach Dungy walked across the parking lot, carrying a tray with the last few things from his office, as my wife continues to emphasize to this day, in the rain! That night, the woman who once defied the hot Florida sun while nine months pregnant to attend a Buccaneers football game was, as she said, done. Done she was in that we were lucky if we got her to notice our shouts and screams from the family living room when she was on the other side of the house on a Sunday afternoon.

She has never forgotten when I took our son to the Buccaneers training camp and Coach Dungy approached us to say hello and thank us for coming. My eleven-year-old son, John Wesley, quickly called his mom from my cell phone and handed it over to the coach, saying, "It's my mom. Say hello." Coach Dungy, who is a big supporter of the family unit, took the phone with a grin on his face and talked to one of his biggest fans, a woman who showed more loyalty than that of Jonathan to David. Since that time, we have moved on. Well, she hasn't, but John Wesley and I have. Besides, Coach Dungy has made his home in Tampa where his involvement and effort to make a difference in the area and beyond can still be admired.

I am sure Coach Dungy is not aware of the marital conflict he initiated on Monday, October 6, 2003, at 9:00 p.m. It was the evening that Coach Dungy and his Colts from Indianapolis would visit Tampa to play the then reigning Super Bowl champions, the Tampa Bay Buccaneers, the team which my wife still calls Tony's team. That night was extra special because it was Coach Dungy's forty-eighth birthday.[22]

It was the fourth quarter, and my wife had removed herself from the family room either to keep from crying or to not allow the godly mother of our home to be seen in a fleshly moment. There were four minutes left in the game, and the Buccaneers were creaming the Colts 35 to 14. I am sure by this time the advertisers were thinking that they had been ripped off since most of the market had turned off their televisions and gone to bed. With four minutes left in the game, a 35 to 14 lead, and one of the greatest defenses of all time on the field, a comeback seemed to be impossible.[23] It was safe to say the game was over. But never say die!

In a living room that had grown deathly silent with a stricken woman standing in the shadows, her nails between her teeth, we would watch one of the greatest comebacks in NFL history unfold. It would be in overtime that Coach Dungy would celebrate with his team a comeback victory of 38 to 35 in a dramatic finish, victory over a team that just a few years prior had dismissed him.[24] From the visitors' locker room there came the sound of rugged baritone voices that belted an off-key version of "Happy Birthday" to a man with class who demonstrated not only how to arrive in a city but how to leave one.[25] As for the marital issues; well, there are some things that should not be written about (haha!).

The message from the outcome of the game is still clear regardless of which team you were rooting for. The message is: Never say die. No matter what you have been through, no matter what the score is, it's never too late for you to get back in the game. The late finish of the cross is a message to you that no matter what you have done or what has been done to you it is never too late. Never say die. Never give up. The Bible is full of second-half champions. True champions emerge in the second half. It's not about what you have been through but rather how you respond to what you have been through. Have a finish that will outlive you. Have a fourth quarter that someone will write about.

Never forget that the cross was followed by a resurrection.

—JOHNNY HONAKER

CHAPTER 5

SCARLET LETTER

HOW LONG HAVE you been wearing a scarlet letter on your chest? Scarlet letters serve as constant reminders of your painful history and refuse to let a failure die. These letters attack your identity and besiege your dream and purpose. They remind you of your hurt and brokenness and insist on being worn for the rest of your life. Your scarlet letter has brought you much shame and humiliation as it did for Hester Prynne. It keeps you tied to your trauma and trussed to the failures in your life.

When you begin the journey from brokenness to wholeness, a time comes when you remove the scarlet letter and refuse to let anyone put it back on you again. You refuse the letters and the hate mail that is sent to assault the work of the Holy Spirit in your life. You ignore the cyber bullies of your dreams and destiny who attack you through social media. You cease to accept the self-addressed letters from the quondam things that God touched and delivered in your life.

The burden and weight of a scarlet letter will attempt to fasten itself upon your chest, not only as a result of your failures but from the trauma and broken places that have accumulated in your heart. Its purpose is to alter and distract from the plan that God has for you.

THE LETTER A

The Scarlet Letter is a timeless classic written by American author Nathaniel Hawthorne that was first published in 1850.[1] The story takes place in the seventeenth-century Puritan establishment of Boston, Massachusetts. The central character of the book is Hester Prynne, a woman who has an affair from which she conceives a daughter. Hester tries to break away from her pain and brokenness to create a new life. She finds it difficult to move past her shame because she is forced to wear a scarlet A upon her chest. The scarlet A identifies her as an adulteress and binds her to her failure. The scarlet letter is a reminder of her painful solitude.

Not to take away from this classic that has found its way into opera houses, theaters, and school classrooms, but the hypocrisy of those who insisted Hester wear the scarlet letter is dumbfounding. If Hester had to be labeled for her sin, then where are the letters used to identify the failures of everyone else in the community? How soon we forget the work of grace in our own lives.

In 2 Timothy 4:17, the Apostle Paul says he was delivered from the mouth of the lion. Paul had passion and a relentless pursuit for broken and hurting people, an inclination from the Bible to modern-day Christianity that would prompt the questions: "Why did Paul have such devotion to Christ?" and "Why did he show such allegiance and homage that was aberrant during that time?" Paul was a man who was misunderstood. He would be thrown into jail and later lead the jailor to salvation. He was beaten and ran out of town, but he would just go to the next city and continue his relentless mission.

Why was Paul's faith so exceptional above all others? He answers the question saying, "It is the love of Christ that constrains me. It's not my love for Him, though I love Him, but when I think about how much He loves me (2 Cor. 5:14). I was the worst of sinners" (1 Tim. 1:15). Paul explains, "I hated

Christians and threw them in jail. I was against everything that Christ's name was upon. I had a scarlet letter upon my chest. To think that after all I had done and the man that I had become, that He would come and deliver me out of the mouth of the lion. I love Him, but it's not my love for Him. It is His love for me that constrains me. When I think about how good He has been to me and how He has loved me, delivered me, and removed the scarlet letter from my chest, how can I not give my all for Him? How can I not show the same grace and mercy that has been given to me to those who are hurting and broken?" (1 Tim. 1:14). Like the Apostle Paul, you are a recipient of such grace and have been pulled from the mouth of the lion. How can you not offer grace to others? How can you inflict the weight and burden of a scarlet letter upon another after being gifted with such mercy?

In John 8:1–12, casuistry is addressed when a woman who has been caught in the act of adultery is flung at the feet of Jesus. The religious posse stamped the scarlet letter A on her chest and pushed her through the streets. The woman, in shame of her failure and brokenness, could not lift her head to look into the eyes of Jesus. She offered no defense or excuse for her sin, and she didn't cast blame or demand that the other party be persecuted. She lay in the street with the scarlet letter that the religious hypocrites had placed upon her. Jesus's response is profound and hermetic. Jesus, the Son of the living God, knelt down and began to write in the dirt. He was not intimidated to touch the tarnish of this woman's life. As He wrote in the dirt, He addressed the biblical Puritans who had forced her to walk the scaffold of public disgrace and shame. Jesus said, "Let the one who has never sinned throw the first stone!" (v. 7, NLT). What Jesus wrote in the dirt was left to our imaginations. One by one, the accusers dropped their stones and walked away. However, Jesus's work was not yet complete. He spoke and asked the woman, "Where are your accusers?" (v. 10, NLT). She replied, "There are none." Jesus then said, "Neither do I condemn you" (v. 11). He replaced her disgrace with His grace and removed the scarlet letter that her failure had brought upon her. When you bring your failure to Jesus, His blood and grace will remove your scarlet letter. Don't let anyone ever put it back on you again.

Don't Touch What Jesus Has Covered with His Blood

In the Old Testament, the ark of the covenant was a symbol of the presence of God; and the mercy seat, which was seated upon the ark, was a symbol of God's mercy and grace. It was the throne of Israel, highly reverenced and esteemed. In 1 Samuel 4, the Philistines defeated Israel in battle. In the defeat, they captured and took possession of the ark. The ark of the covenant in the hands of the Philistines brought destruction and calamity. Confused about how the ark had brought such blessing to the people of Israel but such adversity to them, the Philistines transported it from city to city with the same destructive outcome each time.

In 1 Samuel 6, the ark was taken to the community of Beth Shemesh. Thousands came for a fleeting look at the ark that had such a reputation. Of the many who would keep their distance, there were a few imprudent men who came and lifted the lid of the mercy seat to peek inside. This angered God and brought judgment upon the men and they fell over dead. God was sending a message: "Don't ever touch what I have put under the blood. Don't ever expose what I have shown grace. Don't ever try to put back on someone what My blood has taken away." It is dangerous to put a scarlet letter on a person whom God has redeemed and set free.

We see God's resolution on this contention. Noah was a righteous and blameless man. God would speak to him and assign him the preposterous task of building an ark, an undertaking that drew much criticism from people who had never seen rain, not to mention a flood. Noah would demonstrate his character and tenacity by completing the commission of the construction of the ark. It would serve God's purpose and silence Noah's critics and naysayers. (See Genesis 6–9:19.)

In Genesis 9:21, we see the vulnerability of God's elect. Noah, the godly man and father, lay intoxicated and unclothed in his tent. What happened next doesn't excuse the behavior and responsibility of Noah but draws attention to the act of touching someone's failure. The text gives great insight as the reactions of Noah's sons in the exposure of their father's impropriety are recounted.

Ham, Noah's youngest son, entered the tent of his father and exposed his nakedness and failure. Ham did nothing to protect his father from shame and embarrassment. He had no compassion for his failure and no remorse or grief over the brokenness of his father. Ham didn't cover his father but chose to leave him exposed. He left the tent laughing and carelessly sharing with his brothers and others about the inebriated nakedness of his father (vv. 20–22).

When Shem and Japheth, Ham's brothers, approached the tent of their father's scarlet letter, they did so with great discretion and veneration. They walked in backwards, careful not to expose their father's vulnerability or touch his dignity and privacy. In reverence and respect, the honorable sons covered the nakedness of their father (v. 23). They were hurting for him. They were feeling his shame. Their eyes were wet with tears, not in blame but in sadness of the public mockery of his scarlet letter. His vulnerability would be exploited by his haters. Shem and Japheth didn't see the humor in someone else's failure, especially that of their own father, a man they refused to define by his folly. It brought them no joy that one of God's elite had fallen and was suffering.

> When you are down, you will never forget the man who gave you the boot and the man who gave you a hand.
>
> —C. C. HONAKER

God would leave the correction of His servant Noah for the moment. He would first address the reaction of the sons to the scarlet letter of their father. Of greater interest at the time was their response to the pain and failure of another. As a spectator, God would observe how the wounded and hurting would be treated. He watched intently to witness who would offer the hand and who would administer the boot. His judgment would be clear and without question. He is a defender of the weak. His judgment falls on those who prey on the vulnerable. Ham would be cursed and serve as the lowest of servants. His mercilessness would not only affect him but his descendants and nation. As for Shem and Japheth, they and their descendants would be blessed and given favor for honoring their father and representing the heart of God in the treatment of the vulnerable.

There are those who have no remorse and feel no burden when they hear that one of God's warriors has fallen. They view the occurrence as an opportunity to capitalize off of scattered sheep and draw a crowd to a ministry and church that is too weak and lacks the anointing to do so any other way. Pity the sheep that starve feeding from such pastures.

Phoenix First Assembly of God is a church with a heart because they have a pastor with a heart. Pastor Tommy Barnett has a tenderness and compassion for hurting and broken people.[2] He has given a hand to thousands across America—from the largest stages to the lowest and forgotten ghettos and slums of the inner city, a community with no shortage of broken men and women. Barnett's empathy was no more apparent than when fellow minister Jim Bakker was hurting and broken. Bakker had found no compassion and had experienced his share of the boot. He would find a hand of love and acceptance when he needed it most from Pastor Tommy Barnett, a true general of the faith. Jim Bakker, with the assistance of the Holy Spirit, would arise from the ashes of his brokenness, be healed and made whole. Bakker would protect his heart from the remembrance of those who gave him the boot and cherish the thoughts of those who gave a hand when he needed it the most.[3]

When life knocks you down and punches you so hard your lungs empty and you lose the ability to breathe, when you feel alone and isolated, when the scarlet letter is heavy upon your chest, when you find yourself in this state, there are two things you will never forget: those who gave you the boot and those who gave you a hand. Those who gave you the boot believed that you lost your value and were no longer a contributor to their cause and agenda.

When Jesus came riding into Jerusalem on the back of a burro, the people were waving palm branches and singing "Hosanna" (John 12:12). The closer He got to His cross, the thinner the crowd became (Mark 14:50). The cross is a lonely place. There will be times in your journey from brokenness to wholeness when you will feel completely alone. You will become angry because you feel abandoned and have cruel, self-inflicted thoughts that ask, "Where did everyone go?" Your brokenness will release the poison from the inside of you that only contributes to your bitterness and resentment. You will be like a man awaking from a violent dream, swinging at everything and everyone, including the non-boot-wearing bystanders who are innocent barring their lack of discernment of your pain.

Don't allow the memory of the boot stompers to overshadow those who reached out a hand, those who saw something in you that you could not see in yourself, those who were not intimidated or frightened by your defensive insecurities. Their extended hands would not allow the scarlet letter to become your identity. In 1980, in the city of Miami, there was a woman who desperately needed a hand, but found none. She would die with a letter upon her chest.

The Letter of Judy Bucknell

Letters become the labels of identity that are placed upon your life to keep you linked with your failures and brokenness. Letters upon letters turn into a tablet with a story that becomes a prison and confinement for your pain and loneliness. Like Hester, you have found it difficult to break away from the scarlet letters, letters that were either self-addressed or sent by your accusers. They are letters that hold you prisoner to the burden of your pain and brokenness.

The tragedy of Hester Prynne is not her failure; it is that she never rebounded, she never became free. She never found wholeness. The fact that her character is fictional does not take away from the reality of the many who, like Hester, live in search of what will silence the pain. She did nice things and completed civic duties. She moved far away, but the miles of separation could not detach her from her scarlet letter of brokenness. Her story ends with her reattaching the scarlet A onto her chest once more: "On a field, black, the letter A, red."[4]

In his book *No Wonder They Call Him the Savior*, Max Lucado shares a story that is similar to Hester's of men and women alike who are hurting and broken and have yet to find what they're looking for. Perhaps the U2 song "I Still Haven't Found What I'm Looking For" is the anthem of the broken and lonely.

In 1980 the Miami Herald reported a story that captivated its readers. It was the story of thirty-eight-year-old Judith Bucknell, a young woman that was strangled and stabbed seven times on June 9. If it had not been for Judith's diary, much of her story would be untold. Her diary reveals the painful and lonely life of a broken young woman. I was living in Miami during the time when I read *No Wonder They Call Him the Savior* and will never forget the words from Judy Bucknell's personal diary that Lucado included in his book.

In her diaries, Judy created a character and a voice. The character is herself, wistful, struggling, weary; the voice is yearning. Judith Bucknell has failed to connect; age 38, many lovers, much love offered, none returned.

Her struggles weren't unusual. She worried about getting old, getting fat, getting married, getting pregnant, and getting by. She lived in stylish Coconut Grove (Coconut Grove is where you live if you are lonely but act happy). Judy was the paragon of the confused human being. Half of her life was fantasy, half was a nightmare. Successful as a secretary, but a loser at love. Her diary was replete with entries such as the following:

"Where are the men with the flowers and champagne and music? Where are the men who call and ask for a genuine, actual date? Where are the men who would like to share more than my bed, my booze, my food....I would like to have in my life, once before I pass through my life, the kind of sexual relationship which is part of a loving relationship."

She never did. Judy was not a prostitute. She was not on drugs or on welfare. She never went to jail. She was not a social outcast. She was respectable. She jogged. She hosted parties. She wore designer clothes and had an apartment that overlooked the bay. And she was very lonely. "I see people together and I'm so jealous I want to throw up. What about me! What about me!"

"Who is going to love Judy Bucknell?" the diary
continues. "I feel so old. Unloved. Unwanted.
Abandoned. Used up. I want to cry and sleep
forever."[5]

When I read a story like the one of Judy Bucknell, my
heart is filled with compassion for the men and women
who are broken, for those who are either forced to wear a
scarlet letter or have burdened their own life with such an
encumbrance. There are people like Judy Bucknell all around
us, people who are hurting, lonely, and broken; individuals
who feel rejected and abandoned. These people wear letters
that represent the trauma and hurt in their lives that won't
go away. The words from Judy's diary speak for thousands
upon thousands of individuals who feel just like she did but
won't speak out.

As you're reading this chapter, you can either identify with
the pain of Judy and Hester or you know someone who can.
Like Judy, you have tried to adapt and silently suffer. You
try to lose your pain in your career and success. Everything
in your world seems to be in order except for what is going
on inside of you. It seems no matter how much money you
make or additional education you acquire, the letter always
finds you. You grow sick of hearing people boast about your
life and how together you are when you can't tell them how
miserable you feel on the inside. Is there anyone who has the
discernment to look deeper and see the hurt that is killing
you from the inside?

LETTERS OF MARY TODD LINCOLN

Mary Todd Lincoln was the wife of the sixteenth president of
the United States, Abraham Lincoln. Many regarded Mary
as the most disliked first lady of all the American presidents.
Her behaviors were misunderstood and uncharacteristic of a

first lady. If not for her letters, there would be no evidence of where such unbecoming demeanor developed.[6]

Mary Todd Lincoln was no stranger to traumatic events, trauma that undoubtedly caused severe emotional damage. Her haters would eventually give her the scarlet ranking of one of the most unlikeable first ladies. From the brokenness and hurt in Mary's life, she provided the needed evidence of proof to their claim. Her scarlet letters would reveal the depth of her pain; pain caused by the deaths of her children Edward, William, and Thomas. These unfortunate events led to severe bouts of dark depression. Mary battled and suffered from painful illnesses. She was declared legally insane ten years after the assassination of her husband, seated by his side as he died.[7]

In one of her letters, Mary shared the only hope that she had was a hope of death that would take her to her husband. Another letter detailed her funeral arrangements, which is not unusual except for the fact that the letter was written seven years prior to her passing. Along with the deaths of her children and the murder assassination of her husband, her son Robert had her arrested as a lunatic and brought to court where she presented no defense in being declared legally insane. As she left the courtroom, she looked into the eyes of her son and with brokenness said, "Oh, Robert, to think that my son would do this to me."[8] Mary Todd Lincoln left behind her story of brokenness in her scarlet letters.

LETTERS OF JACQUELINE "JACKIE" KENNEDY

Jacqueline Kennedy was the wife of the thirty-fifth president of the United States, John F. Kennedy. Jacqueline Kennedy was a woman who had become familiar with brokenness. If not for her letters, much of her pain and hurt would have gone unnoticed. The cruelty of the public eye forbids you to bleed. It only takes you deeper into isolation with your scarlet letter.

Jackie wrote about her distrust of her husband, one of the most powerful and influential men in the world at the time. Kennedy had been trusted to lead the strongest nation in the world but had lost the trust of his own wife. Jackie wrote about her worries that her husband was cheating on her and equated him to her father, who was a notorious womanizer. She said Kennedy "loves the chase and is bored with the conquest—and once married needs proof he's still attractive, so flirts with other women and resents you."[9] The infidelity of her playboy husband, which was an indicator of his own brokenness, would add to her scarlet letter the pain of rejection.

The loss of two babies, one who was stillborn in 1956 and the other who died only two days after his birth in 1963, would only add to her brokenness.[10] Jackie would speak of her loss often. Is there any greater pain than the loss of a child? Jesus understood such loss and pain as He looked down from the cross and charged John to care for His earthly mother. For those who have suffered the loss of a child, there is a special grace that is found in Jesus to comfort your wounded heart.

Jackie's secretary Mary Gallagher said, "I was constantly aware of Jackie's suffering."[11] She would drink heavily to numb the pain. There were days that she would just cry. She had trouble sleeping at night, tormented by recurrent nightmares that caused her to awaken screaming. She was bleeding inside and battling with thoughts of suicide.[12]

Jackie, like Mary Todd Lincoln, was seated beside her presidential husband when he was murdered. The trauma in the lives of these two first ladies that occurred from these horrific events gives reason to their struggle for sanity. For Jackie, a newly kindled love for her husband added to her pain. There were signs that their marriage was getting stronger as a result of love instead of an arrangement for political purposes.[13] The hope of what could have been was taken from her when the cowardly Lee Harvey Oswald shot

President Kennedy from the sixth floor window of the school book depository building.[14]

In a letter Jackie wrote after her husband's assassination, she penned, "I am so bitter against God."[15] Jackie then tried to rationalize this statement, writing, "I think God must have taken Jack to show the world how lost we would be without him, but that is a strange way of thinking to me—and God will have a bit of explaining to do if I ever see him."[16] Like Mary Todd Lincoln, Jacqueline Kennedy would leave her story of brokenness in her scarlet letters.

HATE MAIL

You have been carrying around hate mail with you for years, mail that has stolen your joy and peace, scarlet letters that have assaulted your self-worth. This hate mail has delivered you a new identity that you signed for. In Colossians, the Apostle Paul speaks of the hate mail shredder of the cross: "Blotting out the handwriting of ordinances that was against us, which was contrary to us, and took it out of the way, nailing it to his cross" (Col. 2:14, KJV).

In Roman crucifixion the condemned prisoner, bearing a crossbeam, was led to his place of execution. He would be preceded by a public crier who would announce his crime. His primary charge was written on a tablet, a scarlet letter, which also preceded him and was finally fixed to the cross that he was to be crucified on. As Jesus's cross was lifted, His crime, His claim to be King of the Jews, could be seen handwritten on a sign above His head.

The scarlet letters that have been placed over your head represent your trauma and brokenness. They are reminders of past offenses and failures. These letters record the things that have brought you much shame and grief. They are citations preceded by public criers who announce your failures and brokenness to the world. They are notes that you have cried rivers of tears over in solitude.

The message of Jesus is to bring the scarlet letters that are against you and nail them to the cross. Bring your pain and your hurt; bring the trauma that has brought great brokenness and dysfunction in your life. Nail them to the cross. Bring your failure and shame and nail them to His cross. Take the hate mail and nail it to the cross. Take the divorce papers and secure them to the cross. Take the death certificate of your loved one and nail it to the cross. Take every rejection letter of your dream and secure them to the cross. Get rid of the hate mail, all the clippings of your hurt and failures, articles that come out of your pocket and pull you back every time you attempt to move forward.

Keep some positive mail in your pocket, even if you have to write it to yourself. You need mail that speaks to your hope and destiny. David encouraged himself (1 Sam. 30:6, KJV). Abraham Lincoln, sixteenth president of the United States, carried a newspaper clipping in his pocket that said he was a great leader. When he doubted himself or needed encouragement, he would pull the clipping from his pocket and read it to be uplifted.[17] Encourage yourself. Take a selfie and believe in you. Write yourself a love letter. Address your potential and dreams that have become stagnate. Summon yourself to the greatness that God has placed on the inside of you. Submerge yourself in God's Word, so His purpose and plan for your life can be resuscitated.

His cross is a place for you to take your shattered and broken life. He removes the scarlet letter from your chest and nails it to His cross. He stamps your letter with His blood, paying your debt in full. He deals strongly with your accusers as their stones fall to the ground.

SCARLET—LET SCAR

The only thing manmade in heaven is Jesus's scars. They are beautiful and remind us of His love and grace. When my mother would catch me touching and picking at my wounds as a child, she would say, "Quit touching it. Stop picking at it or it's not going to heal." Let your wounds heal, let them scar. Quit touching your wounds. Take your hands off of your hurt and let those places heal and scar. I have many scars on my body, each of them a reminder of the places where I was injured. I can point them out and share the story of each one. There is emotional scarring in my life as well that has a story of its own.

A scar is the sign that a wound has healed. Your wounds are going to heal. Once they become scars, you will know that you are whole. Scars no longer bleed. There is only pain in the memory of the hurt. Your scars will become beautiful to you. They will be a reminder of your journey from brokenness to healing. Your scars come with a story that you can share to aid in the healing of others.

Nathaniel Hawthorne, the author of the masterpiece *The Scarlet Letter*, was inspired by his wounds that had healed and scarred.[18] Nathaniel was acquainted with brokenness most of his life. On the day he lost his job at the customs house in Salem, it was just another wound of many. Nathaniel was discouraged and stricken with fear. His self-worth assaulted, he did not know what he was going to do next. In shame and embarrassment, he went home and broke the news to his wife. Unsure of how she would respond, he was shocked when she pulled out a pen and some paper and a drawer full of money she had been saving and said, "Now you can write your book."[19] It would be on that very day that Nathaniel Hawthorne would begin writing *The Scarlet Letter*. During the process of writing the book, his mother, Elizabeth Hawthorne, died, and he slipped into a deep depression. He continued to write despite the depression, completed the book, and published it in 1850.[20]

This book is dedicated to the Judy Bucknells and Hester Prynnes in this world and to those who sit in churches and have offices with your names on the door. It's for those who

pay your bills and have great credit scores and for those who
have character and integrity and love Jesus but are broken
and hurting on the inside. It's getting harder and harder to
do what you're supposed to do. It's becoming more difficult
to do the right thing. There is a message in this book for you.
The message will lead you on a journey from brokenness to
wholeness and take you to a place of emotional healthiness.
Continue to read and highlight the places that the Holy
Spirit uses to speak to you. I have prayed for you as I have
written this book. I have prayed for God to bring healing to
every hurt and every broken place in your life. This book is
a hand that is extended to those who feel lost and forgotten
in the brokenness of their stories. Your wounds are going to
heal and become whole. From your scars will come a story to
aid in the healing of others.

CHAPTER 6

POTTER'S FIELD

T HE POTTER'S FIELD is a necropolis for broken and damaged people. It is where the lonely and abandoned give up. It is the abode of the unclaimed and misplaced. It is where identity and purpose are mislaid. The potter's field contains the remnants of dreams and visions and harbors the living as well as the dead. It is a place that is designated for the indigent and silent sufferers. It is a harborage for the pain and hurt from life's traumas and disappointments. Those who do not make the journey from brokenness to wholeness are destined for the potter's field.

The potter's field denotation comes from the Bible, *akeldama*, Aramaic for field of blood, in Acts 1:19. The potters would extract clay from the earth in this area, composed of rich clay desired by potters for their creation of vessels. As the potters dug for clay, holes and trenches were formed that would be used for burial for those who were not permitted to rest in an orthodox cemetery.[1]

Having been mined by potters, the land would be useless for agriculture. The potter's field then became the location where broken and unusable vessels from the potter's house would be disposed. After every effort had been exhausted by the potter to fix a piece, he would make the undesirable passage from his house to the potter's field to return the vessel to its place of origin. Hence, the potter's field became a resting place for broken and unwanted vessels that had lost their value and worthiness.

POTTER'S HOUSE

In Jeremiah 18, God sends the prophet Jeremiah to the potter's house. In verse 2, He says to Jeremiah, "When you get there, I will give you a revelation." As Jeremiah arrives, he looks into the house and sees the potter working at the wheel. He notices the pot that he is shaping from the clay is marred. It is broken and damaged. He sees the cracks in the pot, cracks that defeat the purpose of the vessel. The vessel, which was created to contain and to pour, failed to be able to do either.

The potter keeps the marred clay in his hands as he works with it on the wheel. He shows no apparent frustration or intimidation by the brokenness of the vessel and no signs of relenting or giving up on restoring the vessel's purpose. He allows the vessel failure, only to begin again with his hands deeply invested in the core of the clay. The clay experiences intense pressure and pain as the potter pushes deeper into the earth. He works the clay with tenacity that would surpass the excellence of Beate Kuhn, one of the most prolific ceramic artists of the last century whose work is known and admired around the world.[2]

The house is full of many other beautiful vessels from the work of the potter's hands. The jars of clay are full of treasure as they serve their intended purpose. The skillful hands of the potter settle for no less than his originally imagined masterpiece, the intended vision and purpose of the vessel as he worked to abstract the clay from the foundation of the earth.

The jars filled with treasure would be clouds of witnesses to the broken and marred vessels, inspiring faith and hope of what they too would become, revealing themselves as trophies of the potter's hands, encouraging their wounded comrades since they could identify with the pain and process of their healing. How could they not show such mercy when abounding mercy had been given to them? They too were once cracked pots that found healing and wholeness in the potter's house.

CRACKED POTS

The cry and prayer of King David in Psalm 31 reveals the brokenness in the heart of one of God's elite. We find hope in our struggles, knowing that King David is proof that God can use a cracked pot.

King David cries out to God in prayer:

> Have mercy on me, LORD, for I am in distress. Tears blur my eyes. My body and soul are withering away. I am dying from grief; my years are shortened by sadness. Sin has drained my strength; I am wasting away from within. I am scorned by all my enemies and despised by my neighbors—even my friends are afraid to come near me. When they see me on the street, they run the other way. I am ignored as if I were dead, as if I were a broken pot.
>
> —PSALM 31:9–12, NLT

There are thousands, including many of my readers, who are currently where King David found himself when he revealed the vulnerability in that season of his life. You're in distress and feel like you're withering away from the inside, dying from the grief of the brokenness in your life. You feel alone and abandoned, not only by your enemies but also by those you call friend. You are deeply wounded by the weapon of rejection from those who ignore you as if you were dead. You feel like the broken pot from the potter's house.

By the leading of the Holy Spirit, this book is ushering you to the life-altering decision of Jeremiah's revelation. Will you submit to the process of the potter and turn away from the wreckage and brokenness inside you to embrace the curative wholeness found in Jesus? The alternative to this decision was too painful for Jeremiah to illustrate as he would allow the text to remain in the state of victory and wholeness with the vessel still in the potter's hands.

The other option is for you to become stubborn and hardhearted, resisting the efforts of the Potter in your life. The declaration of your resistance will result in your living the rest of your life dealing with the wreckage of your brokenness. You will remain neighbors with the indigent, silent sufferers in the potter's field—the field that contains the remnants of dreams and visions that will never come to fruition will become your permanent residency.

DEAR ABIGAIL

On April 13, 1777, President John Adams addressed a letter to his wife, Abigail, and wrote of the brokenness in the potter's field. He penned the following:

> I have spent an Hour this Morning, in the Congregation of the dead. I took a Walk into the Potter's Field...I never in my whole Life was affected with so much mellancholly. The Graves of the soldiers, who have been buryed, in this ground...dead of the small Pox and Camp Diseases, are enough to make the Heart of stone melt away.[3]

President Adams concludes his letter, writing, "Disease has destroyed Ten Men, where the Sword of the Enemy has killed one."[4]

It is not the sword of your enemy that will destroy you

and lead you to the potter's field. The disease that gets inside you is what destroys you. Your downfall occurs when your heart allows the brokenness from your trauma and failure to capture your mind and emotions. President Adams realized that the greatest threat is not the enemy that can be seen but rather the enemy that gains access to the inside of you.

POTTERSVILLE OR BAILEY PARK

My favorite Christmas movie is the classic *It's a Wonderful Life*, starring James Stewart as George Bailey. This film has captured the hearts of movie watchers since its release in 1946. Watching this movie has become a Christmas family tradition, accompanied with popcorn, hot chocolate, and throw blankets while nestled on the couch.

In the film an angel named Clarence helps George Bailey keep the important things of life in perspective. George thinks his life is a failure and is constantly haunted by a false perception of success. His self-worth is attacked, and he drifts into a dark depression. George lashes out with anger against those he loves. The angry, external attacks are the result of his dislike of an internal perception.

Looking to earn his wings, Clarence takes George on a journey to show him what life in the town he grew up in, Bedford Falls, would be like if George had never been born. George quickly realizes that he wants his old life back when Clarence shows him that Bedford Falls is now Pottersville, a slum owned and managed by the greedy Henry Potter, the richest man in town. George witnesses the oppression of families he loved. He personally observes the hardship of those living in Pottersville. George realizes more than ever before the need and blessing of Bailey Park, his vision for a community that gives an option for a better life.[5]

Will you make the decision to transfer to Bailey Park and be healed and made whole, or will you choose to live in mediocre Pottersville? Will you continue to have an address in Bailey Park yet reside in Pottersville? The choice is yours.

OUTSIDE THE POOL

American swimmer Michael Phelps, the most decorated Olympian swimmer of all time, was lost outside the pool. By all appearances, he was living in Bailey Park. He had achieved the American Dream. He had fame and money, drove nice cars, and lived in a nice house. Phelps's address was in Bailey Park, but he was living in Pottersville. He was so broken on the inside that he considered taking his own life. Phelps said, "I was a train wreck. I was like a time bomb. I had no self-esteem or self-worth." [6]

How does the most successful swimmer in history have a self-esteem issue? The world saw his address as Bailey Park, but Michael Phelps was living in broken, lonely Pottersville.

Ray Lewis was a former pro-linebacker of the Baltimore Ravens and a man with many other accolades and accomplishments in his luxurious career, none which meant much to Michael Phelps at this time in his life. What he needed most was exactly what Ray would offer: a friend. Lewis saw a man who was lonely and broken in the potter's field. He had lived there for a time at one point in his life as well. Ray would give Phelps *The Purpose Driven Life*, a book by Pastor Rick Warren. It was from the pages of this book that Michael Phelps would discover who he was. He would find his identity in Jesus and discover a purpose much greater than earning gold medals and lucrative endorsement deals.[7]

He would find what he was looking for, who he was outside the pool. You're lonely and miserable because you have no identity outside of who you are in the pool. Your life is more than an unmarked grave in the potter's field. God has a purpose and a plan for your life that is greater than who you are in the pool. There is a difference in what you do and who you are. Like Michael Phelps, you're going to discover this truth, and when you do, you will leave the potter's field and never return.

AMERICA IS BROKEN

Major cities in America have designated plots of land to be used as potter's fields, a place where the broken and damaged are laid to rest. These burial grounds are for the lonely and rejected. The graves are for the unclaimed and forgotten. Not far from the potter's fields in our cities are prison facilities that house broken, living people. America has more people incarcerated than any other nation in the world. With 4.4 percent of the world's population, the United States houses 22 percent of the world's incarcerated.[8] As we continue to evangelize beyond America's borders, we must also open our eyes to the fact that America is becoming one of the greatest mission fields in the world. The most prosperous nation in the world is also one of the most broken.

Healing and wholeness for America will not come from a political party, from the left or the right wing. David says in Psalm 33:12, "Blessed is the nation whose God is the LORD." What America needs is a sovereign move of the Holy Spirit, from the White House to the schoolhouse to your house. America needs a move of the Holy Spirit from the penthouses to the jailhouses.

BLUE PLAINS

Potter's fields are not just for the unclaimed and forgotten. The remains of those who are deemed unworthy of a dignified burial can also be found there. So it happened in June 1942 during World War II. German intelligence designed a plan called Operation Pastorius.[9] The mission was to sabotage strategic American economic targets, but the plan failed. The six Nazi spies involved in the mission were tried, convicted, and sentenced to death. Their sentence was carried out on August 11, 1942, at six o'clock in the evening. Their bodies were placed in pine boxes identified with nothing more than a toe tag. No eulogy was given, and no loved ones were there to weep for their deaths. Their bodies would be escorted through the streets of America's capital to the potter's field in the Blue Plains community of Washington DC. Their only remembrance, other than that from history, is the city's water and sewer treatment plant that was built in Blue Plains years later over the potter's field in which they are buried.[10]

HART ISLAND

New York City is the financial capital of the world. It is also the home of the largest potter's field in the world. It is located on the western end of Long Island, minutes away from Broadway and 5th Avenue, notoriously the finest shopping and entertainment district in the world.

On Hart Island is 101 acres of brokenness, hopelessness, and despair. Since its initiation in 1869, over one million of the city's broken and forgotten have been buried in the potter's field, an island just off the city's coast.[11] Along with the broken who are deceased, the potter's field has also shared its grounds with the broken who are living. Hart Island was once used as an insane asylum for women and a reformatory for young men. During World War II, the island was turned over to the navy for use as disciplinary barracks with as many as 2,800 servicemen in custody.[12]

Twenty-four-year-old Louisa Van Slyke would be the first to be buried in the potter's field on Hart Island. On April 20, 1869, her unclaimed, unwanted body would be carried to the potter's field.[13] Not one relative or friend would mourn her death. It is one thing to be gone, but it is another thing for no one to know you're gone. It would not be long before Louisa would be joined by others—1,875 individuals would be taken to Hart Island for burial in the first year it was open. Those 1,875 people left no identity or proof that they ever existed.[14]

The broken have been used to bury the broken. The incarcerated from Rikers Island, New York City's main jail complex, dig trenches fifteen feet wide and eight feet deep for the burial of the broken. Reality sets in for the incarcerated as they are challenged with the truth that unless their brokenness finds wholeness, they might be digging their own graves.[15]

Bobby Driscoll[16]

Of the one million who are now buried on Hart Island and the millions of others in potter's fields across America, there are many who had family who loved them but had lost contact. Isabelle Driscoll, the mother of Bobby Driscoll, was such a family member.

On March 30, 1968, three weeks after his thirty-first birthday, two boys playing around an abandoned building in Greenwich Village would find the lifeless body of Bobby Driscoll on a cot surrounded by empty beer bottles. He had no identification, and no one came to claim his body. Bobby would be taken to Hart Island and buried in a pauper's grave in the potter's field.

Concerned and burdened about her son's troubled and broken life and fearing that something tragic had happened, Isabelle Driscoll decided to seek help in locating Bobby. The medical diagnosis was that Bobby had died from heart failure due to years of drug abuse, but the truth is that Bobby died from brokenness in his life that was never healed.

For nineteen months, Bobby remained a John Doe. His life had not always been so anonymous. Not many years prior, he was one of the most talked about young actors in Hollywood. Bobby was the first to ever sign a contract with Walt Disney. He worked for Disney from 1945 to 1953. In 1949, at the age of twelve, Bobby won an Oscar for his role as

Jeremiah Kincaid in *So Dear to My Heart*, a Disney movie about a boy and his pet lamb. As a successful young actor, he would make eighteen movies in nine years. Of the many movies he starred in and characters he played, Bobby will be most remembered for serving as the animated model and voice of Disney's 1953 box office sensation *Peter Pan*.

In the mid-'50s, Bobby's acting career began to dwindle. He was fired by Walt Disney, an event that devastated the young actor and created a brokenness in him that would never be healed. Bobby's termination from Walt Disney has been disputed, but many believed it was a result of his severe case of acne at the onset of puberty. After being released from Disney Studios, his parents withdrew him from the Hollywood Professional School, a school for young, promising actors. They enrolled him in the public Westwood University High School where his grades plummeted. Bobby became a constant target of bullies and was isolated due to jealousy of his peers over his movie career. Once again, he dealt with rejection, something he had begun to grow accustomed to.

Bobby became more broken as his heart filled with fear and bitterness. He often said, "I was served on a silver platter and then dumped into the garbage."[17] As many who are broken and hurting, he turned to drugs and alcohol to numb the pain, a lifestyle that only plunged him deeper into brokenness.

In 1965, Bobby disappeared behind his fortified walls, constructions that, like many other broken men and women, he built himself. He constructed a rampart to hide and protect himself from the fear of what would only add to the pain and brokenness in his life.

Bobby's mother would contact Merv Griffin to draw from his influence to help locate her son. Merv, who was fond of Bobby, agreed to help. Bobby had appeared on Merv's telethon show when his name and notoriety could generate donors. Unlike many, Merv understood: anyone will come along for a limo ride, but don't forget those who rode the bus with you. Unfortunately for Bobby, the limo was parked and the bus riders had moved into Pharaoh's house and left him in prison to be forgotten. This rejection only added to his bitterness and distrust of others.

Despite the efforts that were made, they were unable to locate Bobby. It would be nineteen months after the death of Bobby Driscoll that his mother would get a letter from the county clerk's office asking to confirm the death of her son. They had been able to match his fingerprints to confirm his identity. The young man who once had a star on his door and autographed photos of himself from stargazing fans is now buried in an unmarked pine box in a trench with other broken people in the potter's field on Hart Island.

EZEKIEL'S POTTER'S FIELD

The prophet Ezekiel walked through a valley of dry bones, a potter's field of dreams and hopes that had died. Ezekiel was walking through the Blue Plains and Hart Island of his day, a field of dead men and women who were broken and never found wholeness. They were buried, unclaimed, and misplaced from the purpose and destiny of their lives. They were traumatized by the rejection and failure that was a result of their visible acne. They were living in Pottersville, ruled by the cruel landlord Henry Potter. Bones disconnected from bones. They were removed from what was needed to fulfill the purpose and assignment over their lives.

Just like President Adams, Ezekiel shares his heart-wrenching walk through the potter's field of broken and cracked vessels:

> The hand of the LORD was on me, and he brought me out by the Spirit of the LORD and set me in the middle of a valley; it was full of bones. He

81

led me back and forth among them, and I saw a great many bones on the floor of the valley, bones that were very dry. He asked me, "Son of man, can these bones live?" I said, "Sovereign Lord, you alone know." Then he said to me, "Prophesy to these bones and say to them, 'Dry bones, hear the word of the Lord! This is what the Sovereign Lord says to these bones: I will make breath enter you, and you will come to life. I will attach tendons to you and make flesh come upon you and cover you with skin; I will put breath in you, and you will come to life. Then you will know that I am the Lord.'"

—EZEKIEL 37:1–6

The question is asked of Ezekiel, "Can these bones live?" Who will believe in the Bobby Driscolls? Who will believe in the Louisa Van Slykes? Who will believe and prophesy over the potter's fields of your city? Who will search out the Bobby Driscolls on your high school campuses? Who will refuse to allow the Louisa Van Slykes in your family to be misplaced and lost to Hart Island?

Ezekiel begins to prophesy:

So I prophesied as I was commanded. And as I was prophesying, there was a noise, a rattling sound, and the bones came together, bone to bone. I looked, and tendons and flesh appeared on them and skin covered them, but there was no breath in them. Then he said to me, "Prophesy to the breath; prophesy, son of man, and say to it, 'This is what the Sovereign Lord says: Come, breath, from the four winds and breathe into these slain, that they may live.'" So I prophesied as he commanded me, and breath entered them; they came to life and stood up on their feet—a vast army. Then he said to me: "Son of man, these bones are the people of Israel. They say, 'Our bones are dried up and our hope is gone; we are cut off.' Therefore prophesy and say to them: 'This is what the Sovereign LORD says: My people, I am going to open your graves and bring you up from them; I will bring you back to the land of Israel. Then you, my people, will know that I am the LORD, when I open your graves and bring you up from them. I will put my Spirit in you and you will live, and I will settle you in your own land. Then you will know that I the LORD have spoken, and I have done it, declares the LORD.'"

—EZEKIEL 37:7–14

God is breathing on you and bringing healing and wholeness to every broken place in your life. God is raising you out of your grave, the grave that buried your joy and peace. He is drawing you out from behind the walls of your tomb that not only locked people out but locked you in. Your walls kept you away from the potential inside of you that intimidated Henry Potter.

Thirty-one-year-old Bobby was too young to stop living. Twenty-four-year-old Louisa was too young to surrender to Hart Island. As Ezekiel prophesied, I prophesy over the Bobbys and Louisas who are reading this book. I prophesy over the broken vessels that have been disregarded and forgotten in the potter's fields of our cities. You will live and not die! Flesh and manifestation is coming to your dream. God is restoring your family as He brings bone to bone. You're receiving the power to stand back up—the strength to walk out of the potter's field, look Henry Potter in the face, and say, "God is not through with me yet. My best game will be in the second half. I get to choose how my story ends."

THIRTY SHEKELS

Jesus would feel the pain of rejection much greater than what Bobby Driscoll felt when his contract with Walt Disney was terminated. Judas, one of the twelve whom Jesus had chosen to be on His team, would betray Him with a kiss for thirty shekels of silver. Judas, along with the eleven other disciples, was granted special access. There were things that Jesus would speak and reveal to the twelve that no one else was privileged to hear. Judas ate with Jesus. They prayed together. They talked together.

Judas would appear from the darkness and not only approach his God but his friend. With a kiss on the cheek, Judas would reject and betray Him into the hands of those who would crucify Him. This act of betrayal would earn him the blood money of thirty shekels of silver. This money would burn and convict in his hands as we can see in the following passage from Matthew:

> When Judas, who had betrayed him, saw that Jesus was condemned, he was seized with remorse and returned the thirty pieces of silver to the chief priests and the elders. "I have sinned," he said, "for I have betrayed innocent blood." "What is that to us?" they replied. "That's your responsibility." So Judas threw the money into the temple and left. Then he went away and hanged himself. The chief priests picked up the coins and said, "It is against the law to put this into the treasury, since it is blood money."
> —MATTHEW 27:3–6

Under heavy conviction for betraying Jesus, Judas takes the blood money and slings it at the feet of the chief priests. They pick up the coins and fix their eyes intently on Judas, baffled looks upon their faces as they ask, "What are we to do with the blood money of Jesus?" Matthew 27:7 reveals the answer: "So they decided to use the money to buy the potter's field as a burial place for foreigners."

The blood money of Jesus would purchase every broken vessel in the potter's field, every vessel that had been disregarded and deemed worthless. Jesus bought the vessels that had cracked under pressure and were unable to fulfill their purpose. He purchased the vessels that had been forgotten, abandoned, and disposed of in the potter's field. The message of Jesus and His cross is that His blood purchases the potter's fields, including the valley of dry bones, the fields of Hart Island, and the Blue Plains. Jesus's blood brings life and hope to the damaged and hurting who are in the potter's fields across America and around the world.

You feel hopeless and rejected. You feel unwanted and worthless. Your failure exceeds that of Bobby Driscoll's because you have terminated your own dream and given up. It's not that others don't see your value. It's your self-worth that has sent you to the potter's field. You believe your vessel is so damaged that you can't imagine the pain ever ceasing. Life has cracked your vessel, which has resulted in a leaking of your joy and peace. Your vessel is unable to contain the treasures that God desires to place in you.

JAPANESE POTTERY

We throw away things that are broken. Regrettably, we throw away broken people as well. We throw away broken men and women who have miserably failed because they are too messy to clean up. Broken girls metamorphose into broken women. Broken boys transform into broken men. We take the broken to facilities for broken people. We remove or throw away what we can't fix or don't understand. We throw away broken marriages and broken families. It is easier to quit and say your marriage is beyond repair than to address the cracks that have made your home and relationship dysfunctional.

Your broken marriage is transported to a divorce court, and yet another family is placed in the potter's field.

In hesitation of being thrown away, you hide. You masquerade in church in fear of your cracks being seen. You hide in your marriage afraid that if your spouse sees your cracks, she will discover that Superman is actually Clark Kent. You hide behind smiles that serve as a facade to guard a heart that has been cracked and broken. You disguise your brokenness with titles and success in fear of not being accepted outside of the pool. You press through life, damaged and broken with cracks that never find wholeness.

In ancient Japan, when a vessel would break, they would not throw it away; they would restore it. The legend speaks of a process called Kintsugi. If there was a vessel that was broken or damaged, they would fill the cracks with gold dust. The cracks of the vessel filled with gold dust would enhance the beauty of the vessel and redeem its wholeness.[18]

You are broken and have been hiding your cracks for years. You fear that if your humanity is discovered, you will be disposed of. Like Adam in the garden, you attempt to hide your cracks from God. Like a crack in a windshield that is not repaired, your cracks will grow, distorting your vision and future.

The ancient Japanese people did not hide the brokenness of their vessels but instead filled their cracks with gold dust. Bring your brokenness out of hiding and allow the blood money of Jesus that purchased the potter's field of broken vessels to fill your cracks. His blood will enhance your beauty and redeem God's purpose for your life. When your cracks are filled with His blood, you will be made whole and able to contain the treasures He wants to place on the inside of you.

CHAPTER 7

SNAKE BITTEN

E VERY YEAR 8,000 people are bitten by venomous snakes in the United States. Of the 8,000 snake bites, a small percentage will be fatal; about a dozen people a year will die from a poisonous snake bite, most of them refusing or not seeking treatment.[1] In a population of close to 325 million people in the US, with only 8,000 annual snake bites from which only about twelve result in a fatal ending, it is safe to say that you have a pretty good chance of not being bitten.[2] Your odds of survival are even higher if you happen to be bitten but seek treatment for the wound.

The odds are increasingly higher for you to experience traumatic calamity in your life, distress that has the potential to be more lethal than a rattlesnake. If the anguish in your life is not addressed, it can be as destructive as a bite from the viperous family. It's not your trauma or failures that are destroying you and making you miserable. It is how you have permitted and authorized your calamity to affect you. It's that you have not addressed the brokenness in your life. You have learned to live with the pain. You have chosen the route of remaining the victim of a snake bite to excuse your behaviors. You have given yourself approval to be miserable and unhappy. The venomous poison of your debacle rambles through you without restraint, affecting every part of your life with uncontrolled destruction.

There is power to overcome and defeat the snakes that have bitten you and released their venomous poison into your life. Luke 10:19 says, "I have given you authority to trample on snakes and scorpions and to overcome all the power of the enemy; nothing will harm you." The snakes that Luke is speaking of are not the ones that slither on their belly and hiss. He is speaking of snakes that are far more dangerous and deadly. They are the ones that attack your identity and self-worth. They ambush your dreams and vision. Luke says that we have an authority and power through Jesus to trample and defeat the snakes that come after us. These snakes are rendered powerless and are unable to halt God's plan and purpose for your life when you take authority in Jesus's name.

In Acts 28, the Apostle Paul is on the island of Malta. Helping the islanders build a fire to warm themselves, he reaches into a woodpile and is bitten on his hand by a snake. The snake was poisonous, and the islanders expected him to die; but in verse 5, we read: "But Paul shook the snake off into the fire and suffered no ill effects."

WHAT BIT YOU?

The snake that bit Paul was identified by the islanders as poisonous; so naturally they expected Paul to die, not survive. You have been bitten by trauma in your life. You have been bitten by failures that resulted from bad decisions and poor judgment. The court of public opinion does not expect you to survive. Worse than their lack of confidence in your survival is the fact that you can't imagine ever retrieving what has been lost through the bite. The miracle on the island of Malta was that Paul survived the snake bite. As hopeless as it may seem right now, you will recover.

When I was a young boy, I spent many hours playing

with my friend Edward in our cow pasture. We enjoyed many days exploring the area and throwing rocks into the creek that ran through the property. One sunny day, our play was interrupted by an Eastern diamondback rattlesnake. Our failure to heed the snake's warning rattle resulted in Edward being bitten. Our response to the bite was not the advised procedure in snake bite protocol. Having never read what to do in the event of a snake bite, combined with our youthfulness, we did what came natural and ran. Regardless of the immaturity of our ages, we had enough sense to seek immediate help for Edward's bite. Summoned by a 911 call, an emergency team quickly arrived with flashing lights and sirens, which drew quite a crowd of onlookers. The team was well equipped and trained, but first they needed the assistance of my friend to properly treat his bite. The question they asked Edward, and then asked me for confirmation, was, "What bit you?" The antidote for the snake bite was awaiting authorization to be able to counteract the poison that had been released into my friend's bloodstream. With a positive identification, the counteragent was administered and quickly began to work to bring healing and wholeness to Edward's body.

The answer to the EMT's question would be vital to Edward's healing process. There are many venomous snakes whose bites can be destructive and fatal if not identified and counteracted with the correct antidote. The African black mamba has enough venom to kill ten men with a single bite.[3] The Australian death adder's bite can result in death in merely six hours.[4] The Philippine cobra doesn't even have to bite to poison a human; it can spit venom from up to nine feet that can cause death within thirty minutes.[5]

SNAKE LINE

When looking to purchase property, early American settlers would ask the owners of the land if it was above the snake line. The snake line was an invisible boundary that separated land with snakes from areas that were less likely to have them. The settlers preferred to raise their families above the snake line, which was typically on higher ground.[6]

If you choose to live your life below the snake line, you are more likely to be bitten. The area below the snake line is a dangerous and vulnerable place. The areas of your life where there have been snakes in the past might very well still have them dwelling there. Listen for the hiss and rattle. When you are close to compromise, listen for the hiss and rattle. When you are responding to inappropriate text messages, listen for the hiss. When you find yourself walking below the snake line, listen for the rattle. When you're telling yourself it is just one drink, listen for the hiss of the snake that lives below the snake line. Listen for the rattle of a deadly diamondback as you dip below the snake line with Internet porn.

The hiss and rattle are messages of warning, alerting that you have drifted below the snake line in your life. The hiss and rattle are messages of destruction and heartbreak, messages that you're in danger of being bitten and poisoned by venom that will take you to a place of hopelessness and despair. Listen for the hiss and rattle, reestablish your boundaries, and refuse to cross the snake line. It very well may save not only your life but your family.

Snakes feed on the eggs of eagles, so the majestic birds build their nests high off the ground to protect their young from serpents. When you go below the snake line, you take your family with you. Your marriage and children become vulnerable to the enemy. Build your home on high ground to protect your marriage and children from the assaults and attacks of the vipers.

Dr. Ben Carson, a retired and renowned neurosurgeon among many other accomplishments and accolades, became the youngest chief of pediatric neurosurgery in the country at age thirty-three.[7] He has received more than sixty honorary doctorate degrees and dozens of national merit citations. He has also written over one hundred neurosurgical publications.[8] Of the many contributions to his identity, there is none more significant than his belief and relationship with God.[9]

In addressing the battles and storms that we encounter in life, Dr. Carson once commented on eagles on his Facebook page.[10] An eagle does not fight a snake on the ground. They lift snakes up off the ground and into the air and then release them midair, so they fall back to the earth. A snake has no stamina, power, or balance in the air. While on the ground, snakes are deadly, wise, and powerful; but in the air, they are useless, weak, and vulnerable. Take your fight to the spiritual realm through prayer. When you are in the spiritual realm, God takes charge. Don't fight in the physical realm. Instead, change ground like an eagle. You will be assured a clean victory. Identify the snake line in your life and refuse to pass beyond the boundaries where you become vulnerable and disadvantaged.

EAGLE CHRISTIANS

The Bible uses the analogy of Christians as eagles. Colossians 3:1 commands us to set our hearts and affections on things above. You're an eagle Christian. Eagles love high places. They have affection for the sky. They love the mountains and tall trees. Isaiah 40:31 states that eagles mount up (KJV).

When I was a young boy, we had chickens on our farm. I would chase them all around the yard to put them back into their pens when they had escaped. I noticed the chickens would get just a few feet off the ground trying to fly only to return to the earth again. If you put a buzzard in a cage that is six to eight feet high with no top, he will remain captive because he cannot mount up. Oftentimes you feel like the chicken. No matter how hard you try, you only get a few feet off the ground only to fall back into your pain and brokenness. You feel like the buzzard, caged and held captive by your failures, struggles, and lack of ability to break free from the horror of what you created. But you're not a chicken or buzzard Christian; you are an eagle Christian. You were not created to live below the snake line. Your affections are for the sky. You were created to mount up. You were created to fly.

You are broken and hurting and do not know what to do. A snake has made its way into your life and family. Take the snake into the heavens where he is powerless, weak, and useless. Climb higher and higher until you no longer hear the sound of his hiss and rattle. The silence is a sign that the one who came to destroy you and your family has been defeated.

Shake It Off

The snake that bit Paul came out of nowhere. He was serving when it happened. His intentions were to help the islanders build a fire that they could share to warm themselves and fellowship around. There are those who have been bitten by snakes in some of the most unexpected places and at the most unexpected times. From the woodpile came a snake that bit and attached itself to Paul's hand. Paul shook off the snake and suffered no ill effects from the bite.

Potter's fields are full of men and women who were bit but never shook off the snake. They made bad decisions and fell prey to poor judgment that resulted in moral failures that they never shook off. Maybe a divorce has left you alone and rejected, and you never shook it off. You feel like your life was served on a silver platter; but then you were bitten by betrayal, thrown into the garbage, and have yet to shake it off. You feel like you were bitten early in life, tossed from foster home to foster home only to be released into a world with no one to call family. The anger and the torment haunt you because you have not been able to shake it off.

What has bitten you that you have yet to shake off? What happened in your life that made you unable to shake it off? What was said about you that hindered you from shaking it off? What was taken from you that kept you from shaking it off? You must take ownership of your pain and the situation that bit you. Realize that Walt Disney is not coming back with another contract offer. Understand that the Buccaneers have moved on, hired your replacement, and will not be asking you to come back. Don't lose your destiny over one snake bite. Shake it off and go win a Super Bowl.

EFFECTS

When the snake appeared from the woodpile and bit the Apostle Paul, not only did he shake off the snake, but he suffered no ill effects from the bite. Paul shook off the snake that had bitten him and the effects of the bite along with it. Shaking off the poisonous effects of the snake's bite was just as important as shaking off the viper itself. It was the effects from the bite that the islanders expected would kill Paul.

You tell yourself, "I'm over the trauma. The failure is in my past. I have shaken it off." Yet you get angry if what bit you is mentioned by someone else and you ask, "Why do you want to talk about what I have shaken off?" This is proof that while you may have shaken off the snake that bit you, the effects and poison of the bite continue to torment and wreak havoc in your life.

The poison is destroying you. It has made you bitter and callous; you don't trust anyone. You have given up and forfeited your dream. The effects of what bit you have made you insecure. You have no self-worth. Your heart is full of anger and unforgiveness. The poison of rejection has created a promiscuous lifestyle in which you compromise and do whatever is needed to be accepted and approved. Self-medicating to numb the pain of the poison has proven unsuccessful. Drugs and alcohol have failed to be an antidote for what has bitten you. Shaking off the snake is easier than conquering the effects of the poison that has been released into your heart. The longer it goes unaddressed, the more dangerous and deadly it becomes.

Man in Black

Johnny Cash was a legend in country music with a baritone voice that could cut through steel. He was often referred to as "the man in black."[11] His dark wardrobe was not only a style choice but also a reflection of his perpetually dark inner being. There was a tragedy that happened in the Cash family that affected Johnny probably more than it did any of the other members in the family. Jack, who was Johnny's older brother, was almost cut in half by a head saw while working to earn money for his family. He suffered for over a week before he died on May 20, 1944, at age fifteen. Johnny never got over the effects of what bit him that day. The day Jack was fatally injured, Johnny had begged his brother to go fishing with him instead of going to work, but Jack had insisted that the family needed the money.[12]

He was more than just a brother. Jack was Johnny's hero. He admired and wanted to be just like Jack. Jack was a worthy model. Even at an early age, he was a young man of great faith, a student of the Bible, and a hard worker. Johnny was never able to forget the words his brother spoke just moments before he passed, speaking of seeing angels in heaven. Jack's final words would be a constant beacon in Johnny's life, directing him to Jesus.[13]

Johnny, only twelve years old, would help dig his brother's grave on the day of his burial. By the time of Jack's service, Johnny's face and clothes were dirty, and he had tears streaming down his cheeks.[14] There are many who have said that was the day the man in black was born. Johnny carried the guilt of his brother's death and often wondered why Jack's life was taken while his was spared. Johnny attempted to silence the effects of what bit him so early in life by using drugs and alcohol to numb the pain. The effects of what bit him would show up in his music with songs like "Folsom Prison Blues," "Ring of Fire," and "Cry, Cry, Cry."[15]

Johnny Cash's wardrobe didn't change in the latter part of his life, as he was still remembered as the man in black. The book that he authored, *Man in White*, would represent more of the healing and wholeness that came to his life through his unashamed relationship with Jesus.[16] It took years, but Johnny finally discovered the antidote for the poison from the bite of the death of his brother. On September 12, 2003, Johnny Cash would see the same angels in heaven that his brother Jack had spoken of fifty years earlier.[17]

CARPET VIPER

Carpet vipers are small snakes found in the dry regions of the Middle East and Africa. The carpet viper is responsible for more snake-bite related deaths than any other snake in the world. What makes this snake so dangerous is its slow-acting venom.[18] When a person is bitten by a carpet viper, the effects of the bite are not as fast-acting as the Philippine cobra's, which can result in death in as little as thirty minutes.[19]

Don't mistake God's grace for His approval. You may have been bitten by a failure. The venom from the failure has been released into your life. You may feel as though you are managing the bite and that there are no side effects, which produces an illusion that you can continue on as usual with no repercussions. You believe you can revisit what has bitten you in the past. The venom of your sin, like the carpet viper's, is slow-moving. God is giving you an opportunity to repent and receive grace. His grace must not be mistaken for approval.

What makes the carpet viper one of the deadliest snakes in the world is its slow-acting venom that can be deceiving and taken for granted. The venom of what bit you and caused brokenness in your life is slow-moving because the trauma occurred years ago, and you thought you shook it off. But the venom has gradually affected many areas of your life. Regardless of what bit you and the circumstances that brought you brokenness, you need an antidote, a counteragent to the venom that has poisoned your life.

ANTIDOTE

There is an antidote for what has bitten you. There is a cure for what has caused you such pain and suffering. There is healing for what has driven you to shed rivers of tears. The antidote, the counteragent, for the poison released into your life that was meant for destruction and ruin is to submit with humility and patiently allow the Holy Spirit to renew and restore you. Commit yourself to the process of healing that leads to wholeness.

COURT OF PUBLIC OPINION

The islanders expected Paul to die. They quickly began to throw stones of accusation. They made assumptions without validation. The court of public opinion deemed that Paul would not survive the effects of what had bitten him. The court of public opinion seeks to predict your ending as well. The verdict is that you will not survive what has bitten you. The court of public opinion might say that your marriage will not survive, that your ministry will wither away, or that your career will fail.

The antidote of the blood of Jesus not only declares survival but promises that you will thrive. In Joel 2, we read that God will restore everything that the locusts have eaten (v. 5). Twice Joel says God will take away the fear (vv. 21–22). Twice Joel says that God will take away the shame (vv. 26–27). The fear of having to wear a scarlet A for the rest of your life is gone. Cain bore a mark not to reveal his shame and scarlet letter but to warn others not to touch him. The antidote and counteragent of the blood of Jesus silences and overthrows the court of public opinion.

CHAPTER 8

COLLATERAL DAMAGE

Y OU ARE SUFFERING from the collateral damage of what happened in your life. The collateral damage may be the result of your behaviors that spiraled out of control. These behaviors destroyed relationships and hurt others, including those you love. You have suffered from the ill effects that developed out of your brokenness that continues to build in pain and dysfunction. Your collateral damage may be from a storm that dismantled your life and continues to bury you in the wreckage. You have been counseled to correct and clean up the mess, but no one seems to understand that the storm is not over and still rages on the inside of you.

As I write this chapter, I am experiencing what Floridians call a hurricane day. What that means is that there is a storm that has been forecasted to affect the area where I live. We have closed the office, and our staff has been given the day off to stay safe at home with their families. Schools are closed as well, and the children are home studying and doing homework. OK, not really. They're actually playing video games and watching TV.

A hurricane day calls for eating pancakes and drinking hot chocolate in midafternoon. On days like these, it's perfectly acceptable to stay in your pajamas and watch continuous episodes of *Blue Bloods*. This perfectly relaxing time is not a dismissal of the threat of the storm. As long as precautions have been taken, such as checking the flashlight batteries and securing patio furniture, garbage cans, and anything else that might serve as an air missile to your neighbors, you do what is advised and stay inside.

As I stare out the window, I consider the moments before a big Florida storm in late August. The weather takes on the look of winter that our neighbors in the North experience. I notice the wind beginning to blow stronger as the branches of the trees start to sway. The sun has been hidden for two days behind the dark clouds that have given Floridians a temporary relief from the high temperatures and humidity. With a slight drizzle of rain, Riverview experiences what is called the calm before the storm.

AFTERMATH

Having lived in Florida all my life and experienced many storms, including Hurricane Andrew, I know as calm as things may appear, they can quickly and violently change. I'm reminded of the aftermath of the power outages and fallen trees, which are minor compared to the flooding from the storm surge that comes from the Gulf of Mexico and Atlantic Ocean. The aftermath of Hurricane Andrew in August of 1992 would be costly, with $26 billion in collateral damage. The storm razed and ravaged 9,500 traffic signs and signals, 3,300 miles of power lines, and 32,900 acres of farmland, an aftermath that turned alluring South Florida into a "third-world existence."[1]

More exorbitant than what could be measured with dollars and flawed image was the loss of life. There would be more than twice the number of fatalities in the aftermath than there was in the actual storm. Accompanied with the loss of life would be the loss of marriages and families. Many of even the strongest marriages would not survive as they were greeted with the aftermath of the storm.

You may feel that you have survived the calamity that impacted your life but are now finding your demise in the aftermath, the ill effects and occurrences of a storm that reached hurricane force winds of opposition. You're struggling against a storm surge in which your hopes and dreams are sinking in despair. You're drowning in the floodwaters of the consequences of bad judgment and poor decisions. You're dodging the missiles of your own debris. You have discovered the messiness and danger of the aftermath of the monsoon that caused you brokenness equivalent to the Category 5 storm of Hurricane Andrew.[2]

As of this writing, it has been twenty-four years since Hurricane Andrew, and the aftermath continues. How long have you been dealing with the ill effects of what bit you? How long have you been struggling with the aftermath of your storm? Remember there is more loss of life in the aftermath than there is in the actual storm. Find wholeness and refuse to be a fatality of your own brokenness.

AFTERMATH OF FEAR

Eventually the storm will come to an end. The sky will clear, and the sun will emerge from behind the clouds and shine once more. The students will return to school, and the hot chocolate will be tucked back into the pantry. When making an assessment of the collateral damage from the disturbance that has dealt a blow to your life, be confident that, at some point, you will face the intimidating enemy of fear. Fear will prove to be your most fierce opponent.

> The dominant emotion everywhere in the world is fear.[3]
>
> —PRESIDENT HERBERT HOOVER

You will find that fear is relentless in its pursuit of destruction in your life. Fear destroys relationships, hinders growth, impedes academic progress, ensnares your dreams, and holds you captive. It deceives you into surrendering your freedom. Fear has come to complete what your brokenness began. In the aftermath of your debacle, be sure to guard your heart from the archenemy of fear. Of the destructive damage of fear perhaps none is more devastating than the paralyzing effect it has on your dream and purpose.

> Fear doesn't want you to take the journey to the top of the mountain....Fear will persuade you to take your eyes off the peaks and to settle for a dull existence.[4]
>
> —MAX LUCADO

The aftermath of what you went through in your life has given place to fear. Your dream has faded, and your vision has become smaller. It is not the water on the outside of the boat that is a threat; it is the water that gets into the boat that causes the vessel to sink. When fear invades your heart and remains, it will sink God's plan for your life. You will settle for a dull existence of mediocrity. In the aftermath of your calamity, guard your heart from the floodwaters of fear. If fear makes an entrance and gains access to your heart, you will quickly discover its destructive and demobilizing ill effects.

John Wesley, the founder of the Methodist church, spoke of the limitless potential of man; not the man who was flawless but rather the man who refused to fear his flaws and brokenness. He said, "Give me one hundred preachers who fear nothing but sin and desire nothing but God, and I care not whether they be clergymen or laymen, they alone will shake the gates of Hell and set up the kingdom of Heaven upon Earth."[5] Edmund Burke, another respected man, said, "Those who don't know history are destined to repeat it."[6]

Knowing your history but living in fear is bondage. Knowing your history and regulating it is freedom.

BLACK BART

Black Bart was an outlaw whose name summoned fear in those who knew of his acts of robbery and terror. From San Francisco to New York, his name became synonymous with danger and fear. From 1875 to 1883, Black Bart robbed at least twenty-eight different stagecoaches. The astonishing fact was that he did so without ever firing a shot. His name and the black hood that hid his face were the deplorable weapons he used against his victims. His sinister presence would stiffen the toughest of stagecoach crews. Under the mask that had struck fear in the hearts of so many was actually a mild-mannered "gentleman" by the name of Charles Bowles. Charles "Black Bart" Bowles used fear as his weapon of choice.[7]

When electricity was newly installed in the White House, it had a Black Bart effect on President Benjamin Harrison. In fear, he refused to touch the switches. If there was no one from the staff to turn off the lights when he went to bed, he would sleep with them on.[8] Soviet dictator Joseph Stalin lived with a Black Bart tormenting fear for his own safety. His home in Moscow contained seven bedrooms. He slept in a different room each night to ensure that no one knew exactly where he was in the house.[9] Other prominent individuals were also tormented with fear. Alfred Hitchcock was afraid of eggs.[10] Adolf Hitler had a fear of cats.[11] Actor Johnny Depp is fearful of clowns.[12]

As humorous as these fears may seem, the reality of the fear that you have confronted in the aftermath of what brought brokenness into your life is not a laughing matter. To you, your fear and intimidation are as real as Black Bart was to the stagecoach guards. When what we fear is unmasked, we are left wondering why we allowed ourselves to be tormented by such a mild-mannered opponent.

SPIRIT OF FEAR

In 2 Timothy 1:7, the Apostle Paul says, "For God hath not given us the spirit of fear; but of power, and of love, and of a sound mind" (KJV). In the Gospel of Luke, when speaking of the things that would become even more prevalent as we near the imminent return of the Lord, Jesus states that fear will increase to the point that man's heart will begin to fail him (Luke 21:26, KJV). The tormenting spirit of fear will haunt you with the unknown, embezzling your joy and peace. It will bring you sleepless nights of mental and emotional stress. The tormenting ill effects will lead to a dark depression that leaves you wondering if you will ever escape its fierce grip.

King Solomon, the son of David, is considered by many to be the wisest man who ever lived. He had a vibrant prayer life and once offered a thousand sacrifices upon the altar. God gave the blueprints of the temple to Solomon. Despite his credentials, Solomon was tormented by a spirit of fear: "Behold his bed, which is Solomon's; threescore valiant men are about it, of the valiant of Israel. They all hold swords, being expert in war: every man hath his sword upon his thigh because of fear in the night" (Song of Sol. 3:7–8, KJV).

King Solomon was so ensnared with fear that he could not sleep. When the king would go to bed, he would summon sixty of his bravest and most valiant men to stand guard around him with their swords drawn. He was a mighty man tormented with fear, a man who would author three of the books in the Bible but was controlled by fear.

Your brokenness, like Solomon's, has released a tormenting spirit of fear against you. It has come in the aftermath of what brought great pain and brokenness. It has arrived on the heels of a great failure in your life and snubbed the grace and blood of Jesus at work in you.

FLORENCE CHADWICK

On July 4, 1952, thirty-four-year-old Florence Chadwick waded into the icy-cold waters of Catalina Island. There she began her twenty-one-mile swim to mainland California. The fog was heavy as she began her endeavor with boats off to her side armed with men who had rifles to keep the sharks away. Fifteen hours after beginning her quest, Florence surrendered to defeat. Her muscles grew numb in the cold water, which proved to be her worst enemy. When they pulled her from the waters, she was only half a mile from the shore of mainland California.[13] From the boat, they could see the land, but from her perspective, she could only see the vast ocean. Later in an interview, she said, "I'm not making excuses, but if I could have seen the land, I would have finished."[14] Two months later, Florence Chadwick swam the same channel and finished in a record time of thirteen hours, forty-seven minutes, and fifty-five seconds.[15]

You cannot allow fear to blur your vision and derail the completion of the purpose and assignment that is on your life. Your brokenness makes you fearful that because you failed before you're destined to fail again. You can no longer allow the fear of your pain and shame to keep you out of the race. The calamity that happened to you can no longer be isolated and hidden by a fear that disguises itself as protection. Every time you consider getting back into the water, fear emerges with a host of arguments as to why you shouldn't. How long has fear sabotaged the greatness that's inside of you? How long have you been dealing with the aftermath of fear? It is time to clean up the mess of the aftermath of what was intended to be your demise.

TAKE FEAR BY THE EAR

On July 19, 2015, three-time ASP World Champion Mick Fanning was attacked by a great white shark. Fanning was surfing competitively in Jeffrey's Bay in South Africa when the attack was caught on live television. Fortunately, Fanning escaped the attack unscathed; but the aftermath of the emotional toll that it would have on him was the greatest concern. The attack was caught on video and quickly went viral.[16] The replay of the occurrence, as with your calamity, would serve as a feed to his fear.

Fanning faced his fear one year later when he returned to Jeffrey's Bay, the same waters where he had been attacked by a great white shark. Fanning would catch a wave and rise above his admitted anxiety.[17] Fear had to be taken by the ear and conquered. The longer he waited to return, the stronger fear would become in his life.

When Moses, the great leader of Israel, died, God placed the mantle of leadership upon Joshua (see Joshua 1), who had not envisioned or anticipated such a high ranking and title. God's biggest challenge with His newly-elected leader would be addressing his fear. Joshua was fearful of succeeding one of the greatest leaders of all time, a man who led the children of Israel through the Red Sea, one of the few who met with God face-to-face, a man who carried the tablets of the Ten Commandments that God engraved Himself down from Mount Sinai. Needless to say, Joshua had big shoes to fill.

In Joshua's defense, I can certainly think of some men who would be intimidating to succeed. When Dr. Mark Rutland resigned as the president of Southeastern University, there were conversations among my peers of the challenge in succeeding such a great man. The search committee was given the exhausting task of finding his replacement, a job that took them several years. The process was not one of procrastination but of respect for the ten years of heart and soul that Dr. Rutland invested in the university.

FEAR OF FAILURE

Joshua, like all great leaders, faced the fear of failure. God taught His new leader how to take fear by the ear. Joshua faced the fear of rejection as well. He knew the people that he was assigned to lead loved and respected Moses. When Moses died, God would hide his grave and limit the people to thirty days of grief over his death to assist in the leadership transition.

Joshua was confronted with the fear of rejection. He probably had thoughts like, "I'm not Moses. They will never follow me." Many questions most likely flooded his mind. Will they serve me like they did Moses? Will they love and respect me like they did Moses? Will my leadership be accepted? Joshua's fear would be the greatest obstacle to overcome in preparation for his assignment.

Joshua was dealing with fear of the future. He was comfortable in a supporting role, but he knew that the burden ultimately had rested upon Moses. Joshua had trusted this burden on such a man of God. He would be haunted by the fear of failure because he was now the man that would be trusted with the burden. Would he fail under pressure? Would he be able to deal with the spirit of Korah that would come to divide the nation? Would he have the patience to deal with an ungrateful people as they questioned God and his leadership? Would he destroy everything that Moses had built and established? Would he fail the people? Would he fail his family and be an embarrassment to his wife and children? Would he fail his God whom he loved and served? Would he fail his God who had honored him with such a great calling?

FEAR OF INTIMIDATION

Joshua had to defeat the fear of intimidation. He and Caleb had spied out the land and returned with a report that it was overrun with giants. The other ten spies who had witnessed the same enemy delivered a message of intimidation and fear. However, Joshua and Caleb reported that there were indeed giants, but they were no match for God Jehovah. These facts had been told to Moses so a plan of action could be created. Now the responsibility was in the hands of Joshua. Fear and intimidation gripped his heart when frequent thoughts and memories of the giants flooded his mind. They seemed to have become larger and more intimidating in retrospect as Joshua took on his new leadership role. The fear of intimidation would have to be confronted and defeated.

FEMA

The Federal Emergency Management Agency (FEMA) is called to assist in the aftermath of a disaster. The storm I spoke of earlier in the chapter has now passed. FEMA is now on their way; the cleanup of the storm is very much needed. A large tree in our front yard, which happened to be my wife's favorite, has been uprooted and is now lying on the ground. The sound of chainsaws and bucket trucks is an indicator that the cleanup of the aftermath is underway.

God assisted His newly assigned leader with support greater than FEMA's. With God's advocacy, Joshua took fear by the ear. In the first three chapters of Joshua, God rid his new leader of the threat of fear. He continued to instruct and encourage Joshua to be courageous and fear not. He assured His intimidated leader that as He was with Moses, He would also be with him (Josh. 1:5, 9). He told Joshua that no one would be able to stand against him all the days of his life (v. 5). He assured Joshua of victory in every place and territory he entered (vv. 3, 5, 7–8).

In chapter 3 of Joshua, God told him that He would exalt and magnify him in the eyes of Israel (v. 7). He instructed Joshua to have the men who carried the ark of the covenant stand in the Jordan River (v. 8). When they did so, the waters parted, and Joshua stood with the presence of God as the children of Israel passed through the Jordan (vv. 15–17). The twelve stones that the Lord instructed Joshua to bring with them from the Jordan were not only a memorial to their descendants but also a reminder to Israel that Joshua was their leader (Josh. 4).

Joshua's fear was confronted when God endorsed him with His approval in front of the whole nation of Israel. When the noticeable hand of God was on Joshua, the people of Israel took notice, and word spread to the enemies that there was no void in their leadership. Instead, the God of Israel Himself raised up Joshua to lead His people.

Fear is one of the effects that resulted from what bit you. You may have been able to shake off the snake that bit you, but the ill effects and aftermath of fear have been tormenting you for years. God's answer to your fear is found in the confrontation of His leader, Joshua. God offers to you the same promise and commitment of His presence. As He was with Moses and Joshua, He will also be with you. In the presence of God, there is an absence of fear. Fear has no place to manifest in His presence. When you feel fear advancing in your mind and emotions, do the things that attract the presence of God. Shield your mind and emotions from everything and everyone who might feed your fears and create an atmosphere of worship instead. Listen to worship music that summons the presence of God. Fill your mind with scriptures from the Bible that oppose fear and intimidation and promise God's peace and protection.

What God said to Joshua is also said to you: no one will be able to stand against you all the days of your life. With God's hand of protection on your life, no one can touch you. When fear tries to take hold, remember the following verses. Psalm 27:1 says, "The Lord is my light and my salvation—whom shall I fear? The Lord is the stronghold of my life—of whom shall I be afraid?" Psalm 118:6 states, "The Lord is with me; I will not be afraid. What can mere mortals do to me?" Isaiah 54:17 promises: "No weapon that is formed against thee shall prosper; and every tongue that shall rise against thee in judgment thou shalt condemn. This is the heritage of the servants of the LORD, and their righteousness is of me, saith the LORD" (KJV).

Part of your heritage as God's son or daughter is that He will condemn every tongue that speaks against you. Your name and reputation are under the watchful eye of your God. His protection is extended to you and your name. His defense of your name is equivalent to when He rebuked those who were questioning John the Baptist: "I tell you, among those born of women there is no one greater than John" (Luke 7:28).

God will bring you to the place where His hand and anointing on your life are noticed by others, including your enemies. He will bring you to the place where, like Joshua, you stand in the river of God's approval and acknowledgement. His presence upon you will be His endorsement and validation. It will not only be notification to others and your enemies, but as you acknowledge God's call and endorsement on your life, it will confront and defeat your fears. Your vulnerabilities and weaknesses are covered by God's validation. All your fears of inadequacy and fears of being unqualified are defeated by God's approval. Instead of living in the shadows of your fears and intimidation, you can cross the Jordan to conquer cities and defeat enemies. Accompanied by God's presence and promises, you can clean up the mess of the aftermath of what caused pain and brokenness in your life.

CHAPTER 9

THE JUDAS GOAT

THE JUDAS GOAT is trained and mentored for betrayal and eradication. His mission as a turncoat is to become part of the herd, gaining influence among his peers. He lives among them, eats with them, and lies down to sleep with them. He gains the trust and confidence of his comrades. At a designated time, he leads the herd to the slaughter. After leading his compatriots to carnage, the Judas goat is placed among yet another herd to begin a new cycle of deception in order to earn their confidence and support that will make it possible for him to lead them to annihilation. His betrayal of his fellow four-legged companions earns him the name and reputation of a Judas goat,[1] a name originated from one of Jesus's selected twelve who betrayed Him with a kiss for thirty shekels.

Judas goats find their way into places of influence in work environments and families. These turncoats weave their way into churches and places of leadership, maneuvering themselves into relationships and falsifying to gain trust and loyalty. Eventually, the Judas goat betrays and abandons you to deal with the ill effects and aftermath of a Category 5 hurricane. The hurt and pain of a betrayal are not easy to recover from. Long after FEMA and the first responders have gone home, you are left with the cleanup of the wreckage of the storm that sucker-punched your life.

PENINNAH

In 1 Samuel 1:6, we are told that a Judas goat had made its way into Hannah's life: "Hannah's rival provoked her bitterly, to irritate *and* embarrass her, because the LORD had left her childless" (AMP). Hannah was in a love triangle with her husband, Elkanah, and his other wife, Peninnah. Peninnah was a Judas goat that had gained access to Hannah's self-worth. Hannah had won Elkanah's heart, but Peninnah birthed him children while Hannah had been unable to do so.

Hannah's womb had been closed, and the Judas goat was attacking her self-worth and insecurities. In the seasons of your life when it seems that the gate of your womb is shut and there is no fruit or harvest, a Judas goat will arrive to attack your self-worth and self-esteem. The Judas goat will parade the fruitful harvest of Peninnah before you to remind you of the barrenness of your womb.

In a culture that considered the inability to have children a curse, Peninnah's teasing only added to the withering of Hannah's self-esteem and self-worth. Without a male child, she would add no contribution to the legacy of her husband's heritage. Among other factors, this proved to be devastating to Hannah's value and self-worth.

When brokenness comes to your life through trauma or failures, you can expect that a Judas goat will try to invade the pasture of your heart. This betrayer will begin to hack away at your self-worth and self-esteem.

THE JUDAS GOAT IN YOU

The deleterious effects of the calamity and trauma that occurred in your life open a door for the Judas goat to make its way inside of you. The Judas goat will influence and betray your purpose and destiny. It will lead you to a place where your dreams and God's plans for your life are annihilated.

The external Peninnah would pale in comparison to the depredation of the Peninnah inside of Hannah. The inner voice that had gained access to Hannah's heart would prove to be more destructive and lethal than the flaunting of the external Judas goat. The internal whisper of the brokenness of Hannah was having ill effects upon her self-esteem in the aftermath. A Judas goat finds entry in the aftermath of what has caused great pain and brokenness in your life. It bitterly attacks your self-worth and self-esteem.

The driving force behind Satan's relentless pursuit of your destruction is that you are a reminder of what he hates. Genesis 1:27 says that God created you in His own image. Just as there is a likeness of a son to his father, you were made in the likeness of God, your Father. Just as Peninnah was jealous of the love that Elkanah had for Hannah, Satan is jealous of the love that God has for you as His sons and daughters.

The word *image* means reflection. God created you as His reflection in the world. With the creation of man, Satan would begin to inquire of God's purpose behind this siring that was receiving such regard and affection. God would illuminate heaven with enlightenment that man would be a reflection of Himself in the world. Man would emulate their God before the universe. Humanity would honor and worship their God. Worship, which once had been Satan's assignment and purpose in heaven before his pride and fall, was now the job of man. Satan was being introduced to his replacement. Man that God created would worship and give glory to His name. God would design man to reflect His image before all of creation.

In heaven, the Judas goat was studious, influencing one-third of the angels to become allies with Satan. Revelation

12:9 says that Satan and his angels were discharged from heaven to the Earth. They were extracted from God's presence, ousted from heaven, and flung to the Earth by His imminence and glory, Earth where man reflects His image.

In rebellion, Satan and his imps pursue and attack the reflection and image of God that is visible through man. This aggression accounts for calamity and brokenness, allowing Judas goat's entrance to influence and assault your self-esteem and identity. They attempt to distort the image and reflection of the Father in His sons and daughters and silence their worship of His supremacy and dominion upon the earth.

IMAGE BREAKER

Dr. Viktor Frankl, author of the book *Man's Search for Meaning*, was in a Nazi prison camp during World War II. His wife, children, and parents had already been killed in the Holocaust. Frankl experienced the brutal treatment of the Gestapo. They stripped him of his clothes, forcing him to stand naked and vulnerable as they cut the wedding band off his finger. Viktor would say to these men, "Everything can be taken from a man but one thing: the last of the human freedoms—to choose one's attitude in any given set of circumstances, to choose one's own way."[2]

How have you chosen to allow the calamity and pain in your life to affect you? How has your brokenness affected your viability? Has your image and reflection been distorted to a blurred spectacle? Have you become a runaway, leaving your purpose behind because you no longer feel worthy?

INSECURITY

Everyone has insecurities that develop for different reasons. The insecurities that have been influenced by a Judas goat from the brokenness in your life are of special concern.

These insecurities result in a lack of confidence that causes dysfunction and attacks your identity and self-worth. Self-doubt limits your potential, disfigures your reflection and purpose in the world, and causes your self-esteem to falter. You camouflage your insecurities with arrogance that is annoying and obnoxious to others. You feel the need to showcase your accomplishments to others to validate yourself. While you seek to persuade others, you are simultaneously attempting to persuade yourself. Your insecurities are masked with humor; but when you are alone, you suffer from self-criticism and verbally assault your self-worth. Your insecurities drive you to show positivity to conceal your false sense of confidence.

ALEXANDER HAMILTON

Alexander Hamilton was a young man of great intelligence and promising qualities. His distinguishing characteristics drew the attention of George Washington during the Revolutionary War. Hamilton was a forceful, persuasive communicator. Unfortunately, Hamilton dealt with brokenness that had created deep insecurities. He obsessed over his personal image and verbally assaulted anyone who questioned or criticized him.[3] A Judas goat had made its way into his life and had influenced his self-worth.

Recognizing Hamilton's intelligence and leadership potential, Washington handpicked him as his personal aide. In this position, twenty-year-old Hamilton consulted with Washington and created important reports on the general's behalf. On one occasion, Washington gave a mild rebuke and corrected the young aide. Hamilton took offense and became angry. Washington, the most respected man in the United States, tried to smooth over the relationship; but Hamilton disrespectfully refused the attempts of his general and mentor. Washington continued a working relationship with Hamilton but distanced himself out of apprehension of the instability of his insecurities. Hamilton's insecurities alienated a valuable advocate and mentor from his life.[4]

Unidentified insecurities would be the ill effects of brokenness and unhealed hurt in young Hamilton's life. In a span of five years, Hamilton's father abandoned him, his mother died, his guardian committed suicide, and his aunt, uncle, and grandmother passed away.[5] These tragedies opened the gate for a Judas goat to attack his securities, which led to a blinding effect and inability to maintain self-awareness. Insecurity can be difficult to recognize in ourselves. We must identify areas of insecurity, uncover their roots, and begin the journey to healing and wholeness.

SELF-AWARENESS

With honesty and self-awareness, we must examine our hearts and motives. Proverbs 14:8 says, "The wisdom of the prudent is to give thought to their ways, but the folly of fools is deception." Ask yourself the hard questions. Why did I respond that way? Why did I act that way? That is not who I am or who I want to be. Where do the insecurities come from? What is the root of these dysfunctional behaviors that are eliminating opportunities and destroying relationships?

With self-awareness and attention to the signs of insecurities, you can begin the journey of addressing the behaviors and dysfunctions influenced by the Judas goat in your life. Be aware that those with insecurities attack others with insults to their appearance and intelligence. Have self-awareness of the reason why you belittle and find it difficult to celebrate the success of others. Develop self-awareness as to why you share information that assaults the character of others, providing random details to deflect the adorations from those who are esteeming them. Seek self-awareness about why you enjoy seeing others struggle and attempt to use their failures to manipulate and control them. Accept self-awareness that while you have given up idols in your life, you have allowed yourself to become an idol for others, feeding insecurities and brokenness in you. Have self-awareness that leads to discernment about the brokenness in you that has produced insecurities and dysfunction. Identification allows you to confront and conquer.

ROCKY

I love the *Rocky* movies, starring Sylvester Stallone, who also wrote the screenplays and directed several of the films. The original movie tells the story of a tired boxer from a low-income community in Philadelphia. Rocky gets his break with the opportunity to fight the reigning champ as a publicity stunt, an event that Rocky takes seriously and begins to train for with an old school coach named Mickey.[6] I have to admit that I have drawn inspiration from his no-quit attitude in the ring in each of the movies. However, when he began to train and the featured song "Eye of the Tiger" started to play, my endorphins would elevate. I would push away the bowl of popcorn and, on more than one occasion, crack a couple of eggs in a glass, hold my nose, and swallow.

Looking back, the adrenaline rush was quite embarrassing, as it was when I took several students to a Miami Heat basketball game when I was a young youth pastor. At the end of the game, security ushered celebrities who had been in attendance from their seats to the exit. As Sylvester Stallone passed in front of our group, I leaned over the railing and began to scream Clubber Lang's rant from *Rocky III*, which is my favorite film in the series: "Balboa! Balboa! I want Balboa!"[7] As Stallone passed, he looked at me with that famous sly grin, humored by an obvious fan of his work.

Long after the featured song mellowed in my ears and my endorphins leveled, I would rely on many of the quotes from the movie that encouraged and inspired me. It is as though the script was written for those who are broken and being visited by the Judas goat.

One of my favorite scenes in the *Rocky* series is in the sixth movie when Balboa is on a street corner in the shadows of the night, speaking to his son about the challenges he's facing. Rocky gives quite the speech:

> Let me tell you something you already know. The world ain't all sunshine and rainbows. It's a very mean and nasty place, and I don't care how tough you are. It will beat you to your knees and keep you there permanently if you let it. You, me, or nobody is gonna hit as hard as life. But it ain't about how hard ya hit. It's about how hard you can get hit and keep moving forward. How much you can take and keep moving forward. That's how winning is done! Now if you know what you're worth, then go out and get what you're worth. But ya gotta be willing to take the hits, and not pointing fingers saying you ain't where you wanna be because of him, or her, or anybody! Cowards do that and that ain't you! You're better than that![8]

Sylvester Stallone would draw from his real life experiences for his movies. His parents divorced when he was young, and he eventually lived with his mother. It would be what happened to Stallone at birth that he would later redeem for his advantage as his signature grin and slurred tone. A forceps accident during his birth severed a facial nerve, leaving Stallone with parts of his lip, tongue, and chin paralyzed. This misfortune made for a tough start in life and later led to name-calling and teasing by his peers in school that resulted in fights.[9] But the real fight was taking place on the inside of young Stallone as a Judas goat influenced the rejections that were accumulating quickly in his life. His hardships continued into adulthood with a dream that he was somehow able to sustain but did not have the finances to bring to fruition. Like Viktor Frankl, Stallone would decide how his calamity would affect him.

With a script in his pocket and a light bill he couldn't pay, he searched for someone who would believe in his story and not just the one in his pocket. There would be those who believed in his script but not in him. The quest would continue in search for a validator of his value and self-worth. He would be faced with a difficult decision. He had the option to sell out his dream for $325,000 but not be the lead in his own movie, or to take the offer of $35,000 with percentages on the gross profit of the movie and remain the lead in the film.[10] Stallone chose his dream, and the rest is history.

Toxic Poison of Jealousy

When there is a failure or calamity that brings pain and brokenness, you can be sure that the destructive allies of insecurity, fear, rejection, and jealousy are near. You will discover that these four destructive allies are more difficult to shake off than what bit you. At the center of the team will be the toxic poison of jealousy. Jealousy is proof that identity and image have been distorted or lost. We see the destructive nature of jealousy all around us and in the Bible. Unfortunately, with honest self-awareness, you may see the Judas goat of jealousy present in your own life.

It was the distortion of the image of God and of themselves that allowed the brothers of Joseph to become jealous of his coat. A clear perception of God would have brought the realization that Joseph's coat was not the only coat in God's wardrobe. It was not the first and certainly would not be the last that He would give. Their challenge would be to celebrate in their brother's favor and protect their hearts from jealousy, knowing that their coats were being sized for delivery.

When you have an undistorted view and understanding

of your identity and image and know who you are in Jesus, there is no place for jealousy. Instead, you relentlessly pursue His purpose for your life and patiently wait for the distribution of your coat of favor. Drawing from Rocky's speech, identify your self-worth, stop pointing your finger at your problems, and go after the dream God has placed on the inside of you. Refuse to allow the Judas goat to influence you with the deadly allies of insecurity, rejection, fear, and jealousy.

BIRTH OF SAMUEL

Just as God needed a womb that could be trusted with the birth of Jesus, God needed a womb that could be trusted with Samuel. The gate of Hannah's womb was opened when she was at the altar and cried out what God was waiting to hear from her: "Lord, if you will bless my womb with a male child, I will consecrate him for your service" (1 Sam. 1:11). It was in Hannah's suffering, in her hurt and pain, in the barrenness of her womb, that God would produce Israel's gift of Samuel.

In your brokenness and suffering, God will birth a Samuel through you, a gift that will impact the world. It was the credible barren womb of Sarah through which God would produce Isaac. It was the tried barren womb of Rebekah that would yield Jacob. It was the faithful barren womb of Rachel that would gift Joseph. It says Mary was chosen, which means that there were others who were considered. God was looking for a trusted womb. It would be discovered in a fourteen-year-old Jewish girl who would give birth to the Messiah.

In Hebrew, *Samuel* means "remembered by God." By naming her son Samuel, Hannah was saying, "God has remembered me." Through your calamity and brokenness, defend your self-worth and securities from the Judas goat and remember that God has not forgotten you. He will birth dreams and miracles through what now seems to be a barren womb.

SCAPEGOAT

Failure has opened the gate for a Judas goat to whisper assaults on your value and self-worth. The Judas goat speaks in subdued tones of failure, defeat, rejection, and hopelessness. Your dream and purpose are led to extermination by the inward betrayal of a turncoat. For every Judas goat that is released to influence the calamity and brokenness in your life, God has provided a scapegoat.

In Leviticus 16:8, a scapegoat is referenced. On the Day of Atonement, the priest would take a goat and sprinkle blood on his head to represent the sins and failures of the people. The goat would be released into the wilderness, never to return and likely hunted and killed by its predator.

Jesus became the scapegoat for your sins and failures, for your calamity and brokenness. The things that brought you pain and destruction would all be placed upon Jesus as He hung upon the cross. The weight of the burdens and transgressions was heavy as it was placed upon man's scapegoat. Jesus allowed Himself to feel the loneliness and devastating emotion of rejection. Jesus felt what man feels when he is alone and abandoned. He cried out from the cross, "My God, my God, why have you forsaken me?" (Matt. 27:46). It was the first and last time that Jesus would feel the separation from His Father. God's eyes are too pure to look upon the evil that was placed upon His Son (Hab. 1:13). For a moment, the Father would turn His face the other way.

Colossians 2:14–15 says that the charges that the Judas goat brought against you were nailed to His cross. Your offenses have been dismissed through His grace. The power and authority of your bondage and brokenness have been disarmed and removed. His blood publicly shames what shamed you. Through your pain and brokenness, His image and reflection begins to appear. Your life becomes worship of the victory of His cross.

CHAPTER 10

ORPHAN SPIRIT

T HE DESTRUCTIVE ORPHAN spirit embodies the insecurities that have been generated from your brokenness. This spirit attacks your self-worth and sense of value. It falsifies that you are rejected and have no purpose. It deceives you into believing you are unworthy and useless. The orphan spirit dares to attack your sonship through Jesus to distort God's image. Your need for approval and acceptance, accompanied with your low self-worth and skepticism of your own value, is clear argumentation that an orphan spirit is present.

Invariably, your family and those who love you are confronted with the negative behaviors that proceed from the orphan spirit in your life. They become exhausted with the demands to feed the insecurities of low self-esteem and collapsed self-worth. Their reassurance nurses a temporary satisfaction that is quickly snuffed out with the unquenchable thirst of the uncontrolled monster inside of you. Relationships tire of investments without returns, so family and friends retreat from the emotional abuse that continues the vicious cycle of rejection in your life.

SELF-MEDICATING

Insecurities that resulted from your brokenness and trauma have created erratic behaviors and emotional pain that drives you to seek the acceptance and approval of others. This acceptance is used as argumentative evidence of your value and worth, presented to yourself and those who reject you. This approval numbs your pain but only briefly because wholeness cannot be found through the acceptance of others. This emotional anesthetic fades as the pain of your brokenness comes rushing in at the slightest form of disapproval and intensifies your fear of rejection, proof that your self-prescribed emotional medication will not address the issue or bring healing and wholeness to your wounds.

CIVIL WAR

The greatest argument of your value and self-worth is the internal war within you. This is a civil war of difference of opinion of what you want to believe and the voices of your history. The bilingual voice inside you proves to be your greatest debater as he drudges up every failure and blunder. The rehash of voices and experiences attempts to disable your purpose and dream.

Maybe it was the voice of a father who left and took with him what you needed to hear, or perhaps it was the rant of a spouse who walked out and broke more than a vow. Maybe it was the silent voice of parents who left you alone in the world. The utterance of constant criticism and failed expectations left you feeling like a disappointment.

CONSTRUCTIVE CRITICISM

The orphan spirit interprets rectification and instruction as disapproval, rejection, and failure of your value as a person. Correction becomes personal and painful, preventing you from separating who you are from what you do. The ill effects of your brokenness will not allow you to receive beneficial constructive criticism.

An orphan spirit is affecting you professionally. You are

defensive about any correction or advice given regarding your job performance and view it as criticism and disapproval. Therefore, the orphan spirit stunts your growth and development and hinders the production and effectiveness of the company which has employed you. The orphan spirit slowly destroys the gift and talent that your employer initially recognized when you were hired. The orphan spirit not only assaults your identity but seeks to assassinate your potential. It attacks and executes the dream and giftedness on the inside of you.

JEKYLL AND HYDE

The orphan spirit has a split personality like Jekyll and Hyde. It may be viewed as withdrawn and isolated, a loner living in fear and intimidation. Or it may emerge as a boastful type A that appears confident and aggressive. The arrogance and need to be seen reveals that it is a cover and compensation for brokenness.

Jekyll is careful not to draw attention to himself. An orphan spirit is comfortable with his residence behind walls, avoiding the spotlight, and dodging places of leadership. It's not that giftedness and potential is not in you. You defer because of your depreciated self-worth and the sentiment that you are undeserving. Hyde's mask is a charade of confidence and exuberance that leaves some jealous and others annoyed. It's a pretense of an aggressive achiever, a masquerade of confidence that attempts to compensate for insecurities.

The orphan spirit has reserved you a seat in the stands. It may be that the best athlete is not on the field but seated in the bleachers. Your gifts and talents will never be displayed because your brokenness has sentenced you to remain seated. There is no shame in watching the game from the stands or no abashment in being the spectator from the seats, as long as the decision is guiltless in that *you* made the choice and not your brokenness.

Strong, healthy leaders are not arrogant and conceited. They have humility and a heart that has earned the influence to lead.

YOU CAN'T LEAD WHAT YOU NEED

America is in need of strong and emotionally healthy leadership. Healthy leadership is provided by leaders who are healthy. The altering of your diet and addition of exercise will improve your physical health. There are many benefits to prioritizing your personal health. It is advantageous for those you lead to have a physically healthy leader.

Humorously, I have taken the liberty at times to use scriptures out of context. One that remains loaded in my arsenal of scripture weaponry is when the Apostle Paul states that bodily exercise profits little. I have relied on this verse to rescue me from my wife's prodding to go to the gym. The only disadvantage of being married to a woman who is a student of the Word is that she is able to use it against me with the effectiveness of a patriot missile. After a theological breakdown of the text, I am reminded of my biblical hearsay accompanied with the notice that Paul also said our bodies are the temple of the Holy Spirit. After careful examination and the enlightenment of truth, it is clear that the intention of the sports fanatic apostle was not to discredit the benefits of exercise but to express the importance of emotional and spiritual health.

America is in desperate need of emotionally and spiritually healthy leaders. It is propitious for our nation and cities to have leadership that is emotionally sound and spiritually sensitive. It is vital for America's families and churches to have a presence of strong, healthy spiritual leadership. The gifts of a leader cannot take us where their character does not preserve them.

If America is to become great once more, there must be a recovery of the values and principles of God's Word in the hearts and lives of her leaders. Don't be deceived by your great leadership skills and confidence. You may have the entire collection of John Maxwell's and Steven Covey's leadership products but still have a brokenness that is affecting your leadership capabilities.

With careful diagnosis of your leadership practices, it can be discerned if an orphan spirit has made its way into your leadership through brokenness. The disclosure is discovered in your motive and need. If leadership is feeding something on the inside of you, there may be an orphan spirit present. If your motive is not pure or if authority and power are used to control your environment, this may be an indicator of brokenness in your life. If your position from the front is where you find your validation, your leadership may have become a drug for your brokenness. If you need the applause from those you lead or if there is a fear of confrontation and correction of those you lead, don't dismiss the possibility of an orphan spirit.

You can't lead what you need. You cannot provide strong, healthy leadership if you need those you are leading. There is a difference in loving those you lead and needing those you lead. It may be that your leadership began with pure motives, but a calamity happened in your life that brought you pain and brokenness, causing your leadership to feed a dysfunction in you.

There are broken and wounded leaders who need healing and wholeness from life's calamities. It is imperative that you take inventory through self-awareness and address your brokenness. Failure to do so leaves a vacuum in leadership and a vacancy for enemies.

ACCEPTANCE AND APPROVAL

An authentic church accepts damaged people, which attracts the hurting and broken. If not already present, the orphan spirit is sure to make its way into the church. The perfect storm occurs when the orphan spirit arrives in the company of others who are broken and vulnerable from the calamities of life.

There must be a distinguishing difference in the church of acceptance and approval. With the discipline and instruction of my children, it was clear that the disapproval and correction of their behaviors did not mean that they were not loved and accepted. On the contrary, to avoid confrontation of behaviors that I did not approve of and knew to be detrimental would have been neglectful on my part as the influential leader in their lives. With the consistency of healthy leadership and tough love, my son and daughter benefitted and learned to appreciate correction and instruction. They came to understand that disapproval did not mean that they were not accepted and loved.

Churches must provide leadership that differentiates between approval and acceptance. In a day when the church is feeling the pressure of political correctness, the temptation is not only to accept individuals but also consent of behaviors of which you disapprove—convictions that are supported by scriptures in God's Word. The accusation is that the church is unaccepting and condemning, a misinterpretation of the authentic church of Jesus. This allegation is addressed by the church with undeviating love and acceptance of the broken without compromising convictions and principles.

ATTACK OF THE KING IN YOU

The orphan spirit relentlessly attacked the king in the heart of David. From the dysfunction of his perceived birth to the loneliness he had as a teenager to the betrayal of a mentor, his life is a testament that regardless of our calamity, life's circumstances do not have to define us. By resisting the orphan spirit, the King in you will arrive at the throne of God's destiny and purpose for your life.

The repetitive assaults on David's self-worth began when

Samuel the prophet arrived at the home of his father, Jesse. God spoke to Samuel and said that He had removed His hand from Saul and had chosen and anointed a king from the house of Jesse the Bethlehemite (1 Sam. 16:1). Samuel arrived with a ram's horn full of oil with his instructions to anoint the next king of Israel. After Samuel spoke with Jesse about the purpose of his visit, each of the sons was proudly ushered before the prophet for one of them to be anointed king. Shamefully, all of the sons were paraded with the exception of David in the attempt of exclusion by the orphan spirit. Samuel had been tutored in preparation for the confrontation. Seeing Jesse's eldest son, Eliab, and thinking he was surely the one the Lord had chosen,

> The Lord said to Samuel, "Do not consider his appearance or his height, for I have rejected him. The Lord does not look at the things people look at. People look at the outward appearance, but the Lord looks at the heart."...Jesse had seven of his sons pass before Samuel, but Samuel said to him, "The Lord has not chosen these." So he asked Jesse, "Are these all the sons you have?" "There is still the youngest," Jesse answered. "He is tending the sheep." Samuel said, "Send for him; we will not sit down until he arrives."...So Samuel took the horn of oil and anointed him in the presence of his brothers, and from that day on the Spirit of the Lord came powerfully upon David.
> —1 Samuel 16:7, 10–11, 13

In this story, we see that regardless of our circumstances we do not have to succumb to the orphan spirit. David could have easily fallen captive to the assault on his self-worth. David was assigned the task of tending the sheep, a job that was not on the wish list of any of his brothers. In fact, it was a job that would have been given to a servant if the finances of the family permitted. For David's family the finances were not of essence; the shepherd field would serve as a place of isolation, out of sight, and a reminder of his rejection.

The word got out that the prophet Samuel had gone to the house of Jesse to anoint the next king of Israel. David would have to battle the orphan spirit while his brothers were being lined up and paraded, while in the eyes of his own father he was not even a consideration. The orphan spirit would speak to David and say you're not good enough, you're not qualified, and your own father has looked past and rejected you. How could God use you if your own father does not see your value?

We can hear the pain in the writings of David in Psalm 69 as he battles the orphan spirit. He deals with rejection as an outcast among his own family. He was laughed and talked about in his own community. Listen in on David's painful battle with the orphan spirit:

> Those who hate me without reason outnumber the hairs of my head; many are my enemies without cause, those who seek to destroy me. I am forced to restore what I did not steal.
>
> —Psalm 69:4

David was saying, "I don't know why I'm hated and rejected. They lie and accuse me of stealing and forced me to replace what I had nothing to do with." His writing continued later in the chapter: "I am a foreigner to my own family, a stranger to my own mother's children" (v. 8). David was saying that his own father and brothers didn't want anything to do with him. "Those who sit at the gate mock me, and I am the song of the drunkards" (v. 12). David says, "They laugh at me and make jokes when I walk by." He then cries out to the Lord:

You know how I am scorned, disgraced and shamed; all my enemies are before you. Scorn has broken my heart and has left me helpless; I looked for sympathy, but there was none, for comforters, but I found none.

—PSALM 69:19–20

David says, "My heart is broken. I feel so alone. I feel abandoned. I don't have anyone that I can turn to. No one can see the king in me." The orphan spirit would visit David in the shepherd's field and say, "It's true, you are rejected, you are not loved, David; you're a burden. You have no future, so you might as well dismiss the silly dreams of ever being a king. Listen to what your father and brothers are saying; listen to what they are saying at the gate. Believe the press, David. You're no good; you're a mistake. You're not a son, David; your own father does not recognize and approve of you."

BETRAYED BY HIS KING

Not only was David struggling with not being valued and accepted by his father and brothers, but David was also grieving the fact that his king had betrayed him. David had finally found someone who saw something in him. David trusted and made himself vulnerable to the leadership of King Saul. He had been given access and was being mentored by the king. He found someone that he looked up to that was looking back. Validation from a spiritual leader; he is God's man, this is a safe place. David found someone that took him seriously and saw his worth and value. King Saul would be the voice of a father in his life that he never had: "Saul took David and would not let him return home" (1 Sam. 18:2).

Saul made David feel like a son. He said, "Don't go back to the shepherd's field. I see something in you." He made David feel like he mattered, like he was of value and needed. David was given access to the king's family. Jonathan, the king's son, became David's best friend; they were like brothers. David did not take advantage of his newfound relationship. He did not take for granted the access to the king and his family. In 1 Samuel 18:14 it says that David behaved wisely in all of his ways (KJV). David was loyal to Saul, giving no reason for the king to feel threatened. He honored and respected his king. He behaved wisely not to bring dishonor to the privileges that had been afforded him.

The relationship with King Saul would be short lived. David would find himself dodging spears from the same hands that opened doors. The betrayal would not cause him to disrespect his king and his position of authority. David refused to play the victim and allow himself to bleed on those that were under Saul's leadership. He didn't talk about his king or create a following, but rather he chose to continue to be loyal.

Your loyalty and respect for a person is not a reflection of their character but a reflection of your own. The painful betrayal of Saul would once again welcome the orphan spirit to visit David. It was a reminder of the press clippings of the rejection and disapproval in his life. The rejection of his king and spiritual father and mentor would be another devastating and painful place in the life of David. In Psalm 69:20, David cries out that his heart had been broken. David's king would certainly be a contributor to the hurt and pain in his life.

Approval of a Father

I have witnessed over and over again the damage that has been done in the lives of men and women who have never received the acceptance and approval of their father. They can receive acknowledgement and accolades from many different areas and be very successful in life, but there is still the need for a father's approval—to hear their father say, "I am proud of you. I am proud of the man or the woman that you have become." They can hear it from a mother or from others, but there is something powerful about the approval of a father.

I heard a story of a man that was very successful in life and had a wonderful family of his own, but felt as though he was never good enough in the eyes of his father. It was something that he constantly battled in his mind. He did not understand why it was so important to have his father's approval. He had his own family that loved him and honored him. Professionally he was successful in his field. He had proven leadership that had attracted those who would look to him for coaching and counsel. He had a lucrative income and drove nice cars and lived in a home on the nice side of town. Yet on the inside of him there was a gnawing that could not be satisfied. When he heard that his father was terminally sick, he planned a trip to visit. He admittedly said while wanting to do what was right, there was a part of him that was saying, "Don't you dare die without telling me what I need to hear." The money and the success and the love of a family had not silenced the orphan spirit on the inside of him.

A challenge to every father and to every man is this: let the voice of a father be heard. Speak to the cry of a generation; speak to the need of a fatherless generation. Be sure to affirm the king and queen in them.

SONSHIP

Your self-worth is found in your identity in Christ; it's found in sonship through your relationship with Jesus. Many have miserably attempted to improve their self-worth through performance only to find that, when the curtain drops, the person that they take home is not the person they want to be.

David refused to accept the orphan spirit and to give it the power to assassinate the king in him. David understood sonship through the Spirit of adoption. Romans 8:15 says you have received the Spirit of adoption and you cry Abba Father (KJV). Ezekiel 16:5–7 says you were thrown away and cast out into the open field and no one had compassion on you. Then the Lord came looking for you and pursued you. "I spread the corner of my garment over you and covered your naked body. I gave you my solemn oath and entered into a covenant with you, declares the Sovereign LORD, and you became mine" (v. 8). There is no audition, no performance; you're a son.

Abba is a familiar word used by writers throughout the Bible. Abba has the same meaning as the word *papa*. The word is not to be interpreted as disrespect. He is a holy and a majestic, all powerful God; but His sons and daughters who are in relationship with Him through Jesus also know of the intimacy of sonship.

STEPH AND RILEY

Steph Curry of the Golden State Warriors has astounded fans and reporters of the game of basketball with the accuracy of his shot, preeminently behind the three-point line. His performance on the court has earned him the respect of his peers and has attracted media attention across the country. It is Steph's post-game press conferences that have drawn criticism, as well as appreciation, from those that find Steph's now four-year-old daughter, Riley, either annoying or amusing. Riley sits on the lap of her NBA superstar father unintimidated that she is on national television. She grabs the microphone and the attention of spectators and fans with her on-camera antics and facial expressions that grab the hearts of thousands.[1]

The reporters and cameras get ten minutes of post-game comments. Fans scramble to get autographs of their favorite basketball superstar. The number 30 basketball jersey with the name Curry scripted across the back flies off the racks of sports stores across America. He is known as Steph Curry the leader of the Golden State Warriors, but to Riley he is daddy. She gets to sit on his lap; he tucks her into bed at night. Riley has his cell number. While others have to schedule appointments, Riley has access and walks right in.

She is protected and provided for. When I see Riley climbing on the lap of her father at a post-game press conference, though some are annoyed, I am reminded of the relationship we have with God the Father. I thank the Lord for the Spirit of adoption and sonship provided through Jesus and His cross.

CHAPTER 11

JOURNEY TO WHOLENESS

NAAMAN WAS A brave warrior and highly regarded. He had power, position, and prestige. He was an honored military leader of one of the most powerful nations of his day. He was esteemed and admonished as a man of valor. He was credited with success and defeat over every enemy except for the one inside of him. Naaman was haunted by the three-letter conjunction *but*: "But he was a leper" (2 Kings 5:1, KJV).

His armor identified him as a mighty leader; but under his protective covering, he was just another broken man, lonely and afraid of rejection. His bloody T-shirt and the smell of his brokenness were becoming more difficult and exhausting to disguise. Naaman had conquered every enemy but the one inside of him. He discovered that the first step in the journey from brokenness to wholeness is to acquire the courage to face the fiercest enemy, the one in you.

Naaman laid down his sword, removed his armor, and trekked into the muddy waters of the Jordan River (v. 14). He confronted what had tormented him throughout his life. He exposed his brokenness as he stepped in obedience in the walk to wholeness. The prophet Elisha had instructed him to dunk seven times in the river, each dunk required for his healing and wholeness (v. 10).

SEVEN DUNKS TO WHOLENESS

1. Identify

The first dunk is to identify. As with Naaman, you must acknowledge the enemy in you. Falsely identifying your enemy will only doom you to remain a victim of your calamity and a prisoner of your failure. Attempts at correcting behaviors and treating the ill effects of what bit you have proven to be exhausting and ineffective. It is not until the snake is identified that there can be a prescribed antidote to bring you to wholeness.

Joni Eareckson Tada refused to be sent to the potter's field by being the victim of her own circumstances and calamity. She identified the real enemy that was destructive and dangerous to her destiny and purpose. On July 30, 1967, seventeen-year-old Joni Eareckson went swimming in Chesapeake Bay. Joni dove into the murky water, unaware that it was shallow. Her head crashed into a rock, and her neck snapped. She felt a strange electric shock. She was pulled from the water and rushed to the hospital. The team of medical doctors stated that the young girl had severed her spinal cord and would be left a quadriplegic, paralyzed from her shoulders down.[1]

During her first two years of rehabilitation, Joni experienced anger, depression, and suicidal thoughts. Questions of why God would allow this to happen circled in her mind. She begged her friends to assist her in committing suicide. Joni eventually confronted the enemies in her life and found purpose through her faith and relationship with Jesus.[2] Her life is an inspiration and encouragement to thousands. Her story reminds us that no matter how destructive your calamity may have been, your life can have meaning and significance.

Joni learned to write and paint by holding a brush between her teeth. She has authored over forty books and recorded several musical albums among many other accomplishments. Joni stated that there have been many people who have approached her and asked if they could pray for her healing. She says, "I know they mean well, but I tell them if you want to pray for me, please pray for the times when I cherish inflated ideas of my own importance. Pray for the times when I fudge the truth and manipulate my husband to get my own way. If you want to pray for me, pray that I receive the power of resurrection to put to death the things in my life that displease God."[3] Joni identified the enemy in her that served as her greatest threat

2. Confront

The second dunk is to confront the enemy that you have identified. You will have to acquire the courage for this confrontation. Protecting the effects of your calamity and brokenness is fear. Fear has established itself well in your life and has been effective in prolonging the confrontation. It has become the warden of the walls that you erected to keep people out which have also locked you in. Fear of Black Bart has caused you to retreat, surrendering the treasures of your peace and the purpose that God had placed in you. After unmasking Black Bart and discovering the weasel Charles Bowles, you can begin to confront the enemy in you.

3. Trust the Holy Spirit

The third dunk is to trust the blueprints of the Holy Spirit. He will carefully reveal and navigate your journey to wholeness. The blueprints of New York's Citicorp Center revealed the defectiveness of the building and what would be needed to make the building structurally sound. The Holy Spirit will divulge the true enemy that has brought brokenness to your life and lead you in the steps of obedience in your walk to wholeness.

NEW YORK'S CITICORP CENTER[4]

New York's Citicorp Center was completed and ready for occupancy in 1977. One year after the building opened, structural engineer William J. LeMessurier realized the Citicorp Center was defective. Joints that should have been welded were inadequately bolted. With severe winds from a storm, there was a possibility that the building could collapse, causing thousands of fatalities. The building was broken.

LeMessurier had to make a decision whether to stay silent and hope for the best or confront the issue that would cost millions of dollars to repair and possibly end his career. He chose to confront the defects of the building and owned the brokenness. He addressed and corrected the issues carefully; he studied the blueprints and followed the plans and advice of experts. His career was not over; instead he was admired for the courage he had to admit that there was a problem, confront the issue, and make it right.

Your life reminds you of New York's Citicorp Center. The appearance is that you are strong, successful, and have it all together; but you know that you are not structurally sound and have identified your brokenness. You have acquired the courage to confront the damage and will trust the plans and blueprints provided by the Holy Spirit to lead you to wholeness. Your courage is admired as you remove the armor that has served as a facade, confront the stink of the bloody T-shirt, and follow the blueprints to healing and wholeness.

Your blueprints are tailored for your individual circumstance and brokenness. Trust the care and precision provided by the leadership of the Holy Spirit for your journey to wholeness. He will far exceed the expectations of LeMessurier. Your blueprints, though tailored specifically for you, are certain to include the following.

4. Forgiveness

Of the dangerous ill effects from what bit you and caused brokenness and calamity, there is none more deadly than unforgiveness. On July 2, 1881, at 9:20 in the morning, just four months after his inauguration, President James Garfield arrived at the railroad station in Washington DC. Charles Guiteau approached from the shadows and shot the president in the shoulder and once in the back. The president cried out, "My God, what is this?" He lived eighty days after being shot and passed away on September 19, 1881. American doctors of the day did not believe in antisepsis measures or the need for cleanliness to prevent infection. Several of the physicians inserted their unsterilized fingers into the wound to probe for the bullet. Infection ended up taking Garfield's life rather than the gunshot.[5]

The infectious poison of unforgiveness makes its way through the wound of what has caused brokenness and pain in you. The ill effects of unforgiveness will prove to be more destructive and deadly than the gunshot that wounded you. Jesus said in Matthew 18:7, "Woe unto the world because of offences! for it must needs be that offences come; but woe to that man by whom the offence cometh!" (KJV). The word *offense* in Greek is *skandalon*, which means a trigger that drops the trap and ensnares an unsuspecting victim or a native rock rising up through the earth, which trips up the traveler.[6] Jesus was teaching that an offense that is harbored and unforgiven is a trap that ensnares and a rock that causes you to stumble.

The fourth dunk in the journey to wholeness is to forgive those who have hurt you, caused you pain, and contributed to your brokenness. You will need to forgive your offenders and release the offense. You will never arrive at wholeness with a heart that is bitter with unforgiveness. You may discover in your journey to wholeness that the Holy Spirit will reveal your need to forgive God. Of course, God has not sinned against you or done anything worthy of offense, but you may have secretly become angry and offended at God. Like Mary and Martha questioned Jesus's whereabouts when their brother died (John 11:21, 32), you may find yourself asking, "Jesus, where were You? Why didn't You come? I needed You, but now it's too late." Where has God not made an appearance in your life that has disappointed you and left you wondering? What has God allowed to die in your life that has left you angry with Him even though He didn't cause it?

There was a young family who attended our church several years ago. They had a baby who was not yet a year old and was very sick. I would visit the baby and pray for her along with the young mother and father. A short time later, the baby passed. Several weeks later, twenty minutes into the Sunday worship service, the young father, tears streaming down his face, stood up and began to scream out repeatedly, "God, I'm not mad at you." A wave of God's grace and love flowed over that man and across the auditorium. Many lives were touched that Sunday morning by the Holy Spirit, especially the precious young couple who had lost their child. Though their hearts were broken, they didn't fall into the trap of taking offense against God. They will never forget the short time that their little girl blessed their lives, but God saw their pure hearts and later gifted them with another child.

In your journey to wholeness, it is critical that you forgive those who have hurt you. It may even be necessary to let go of an offense toward God. It is imperative that you forgive yourself. You will arrive at a place where you have conceded mercy to everyone but yourself. The contemporary Christian band MercyMe chose their name when the lead singer's grandmother, not understanding her grandson's choice of career, said, "Well, mercy me, why don't you get a real job?"[7] My interpretation of this popular group's name is that

MercyMe implies mercy and forgiveness for oneself. It may not be the meaning behind the name of the six-time Dove Award–winning band,[8] but in your journey to wholeness, let it be a reminder to show mercy and forgiveness to yourself.

5. Grieve Your Losses

In your life, there have been relationships and junctures at which you have suffered painful loss. In the journey to wholeness, you must permit yourself to grieve losses. Your attachment to what has been removed from your life burdens your wholeness. The spouse who walked out and took away the life that you loved is not coming back. The fantasy of what it would be like to have your father in your life is not reality. The collateral damage of your failure has accounted for loss that cannot be recouped. The fatal attraction to your pain refuses to let go and impedes your healing.

When Moses died, God allowed Israel thirty days to grieve the loss of their beloved leader (Deut. 34:8). It would be necessary for them to grieve their loss to regain the strength to arrive at their destiny. They would need to grieve their loss to embrace the fated plan that was destined for their lives. It was not until they had grieved for Moses that they could be introduced to Joshua.

In the Book of Joel, the nation of Judah grieved her losses in sackcloth all night (1:13), and God responded and restored to them the years that the locust had stolen and brought blessing and wholeness to the nation and her people who had suffered great losses (2:25–32). You have questioned if you will ever be alleviated from the pain of your losses. Will you ever know peace and joy again? Will God ever be able to use you again? Was your purpose displaced in the aftermath of your storm?

As you trust the Holy Spirit and His blueprints for your journey to wholeness, you will discover that your best days are ahead of you. Your joy is not coupled in what you lost but in arriving at the place where you cut your losses and trust Jesus to navigate you through the pain of your brokenness to His healing and wholeness. Moses's body was removed and buried in an undisclosed location, sending a message to the Israelites to cut their losses and attachment to what was dead and would not return. Your Joshua is patiently waiting to lead you into what has been promised over your life.

6. Renewing of Your Mind

Your brokenness creates a mind-set and a language of its own. This mind-set stirs up the hurt and dysfunction of the calamity that occurred in your life. This mentality is an attachment to your brokenness and resists allowing you to enjoy the benefits of wholeness. In your journey to wholeness, you will discover that the transformation from brokenness to wholeness will require the renewing of your mind (Rom. 12:2). In renewing your mind, you must recognize the old way of thinking, bring it into the captivity of Christ, and cast it down. To *renew* means to exchange the old for the new. You must learn the new language of wholeness spoken through the truth of God's Word, a language that is foreign to you since you have only spoken the destructive dialect of your calamity since you were broken.

Genesis 37 and 39 tell us the stories of Joseph's struggles and hurt that started at the young age of seventeen. Over the next decade of his life, he would suffer rejection through the betrayal of his brothers and defamation of his character by Potiphar's wife, a woman who tried to seduce him. Being a man of character, he ran, leaving his coat behind. She lied and had him incarcerated. In chapter 40, while he was in prison, he was deceived by the baker and the butler who told him that they would speak on his behalf, but the representation never happened.

Joseph was a young man who loved God; but he was human, and I am sure there were times when he had to battle bitterness and resentment and protect his heart from the poison of unforgiveness. Joseph would constantly have to cast down every thought and bring them into the captivity of Christ. His mind would need to be renewed with the truth and the promise of his coat of many colors. By renewing his mind, his heart remained pure, and he arrived at his purpose and God's plan for his life (Gen. 41). Paul says in Ephesians 5:26 that there is power in the Word of God to wash your mind. It washes and removes the old and transforms by the renewing of your mind.

7. Jesus Glows in the Dark

In 1979, Bill Wilson moved to Brooklyn, New York, in a station wagon with a bullhorn and a Yogi Bear costume in the trunk. He had a vision and a passion to reach the broken of the inner city regions. Metro Ministries (now Metro World Child) was born as a result. Metro Ministries transports thousands of children each week to church from some of the most despondent neighborhoods in America.[9] It was from such a neighborhood that a little girl would board the bus that Pastor Bill was driving as he often did. It was the Christmas season, and this little girl could not allow her favorite bus captain to be forgotten. As she stepped on the bus with a grin of anticipation, she whipped out a gift from behind her back that was wrapped in old newspapers and covered with scotch tape. She excitedly pronounced, "It's for you, Pastor Bill!" He smiled, said thank you, and went to set the gift down to open later. However, the determined little elf insisted that he open it immediately as a crowd had gathered at the front of the bus. Not wanting to appear ungrateful, he pulled the bus over and began to open the gift that he would never forget. Under the torn sheets of last week's sports page and comics was an old figurine of Jesus that was broken but identifiable. Pastor Bill enthusiastically thanked the little girl for her beautiful present. As the children were making their way back to their seats, he reached to engage the transmission, but the little girl giggled with excitement and let out a squeal. With descriptive instruction, she told Pastor Bill to cover the figurine with his hands and then asked, "Do you see it, Pastor Bill? Do you see it? Jesus glows in the dark!"[10] The gift would serve as a reminder of why he had given his life to the dark streets of the inner city. We serve a Jesus that glows in the dark.

The seventh dunk is to expose your brokenness to a Jesus that heals and is not intimidated by the dark, messy places in your life. The Jesus that glows in the darkness of America's inner city is the Jesus that will glow in the inner core of your heart. Psalm 34:18 says, "The LORD is close to the brokenhearted and saves those who are crushed in spirit." It is this Jesus who would come near the broken in John 5 at the pool of Bethesda. He would quickly address the purpose of His visit with a man who had been broken for thirty-eight years. Jesus would say to this man what He says to each reader: "Do you want to be whole? Do you want Me to touch the insecurities that have developed during thirty-eight years of brokenness? Do you want Me to touch your self-worth that has been deflated by being made to crawl for thirty-eight years? Do you want Me to speak to the rejection that has plagued you? Do you want Me to tear down the walls that have hidden you in fear? And, by the way, I can heal your legs too!"

Your journey to wholeness starts when you allow the wind of the Holy Spirit to blow upon every broken place in your life. This wind moved upon the face of the Earth in Genesis. This wind blew on Ezekiel's valley of dry bones. This wind moved upon the womb of Mary in the Gospels. This wind blew through the Upper Room on the Day of Pentecost. It is this wind, the wind of the Holy Spirit that will blow over every broken place in your life and bring you to a place of wholeness. Psalm 147:3 says, "He heals the brokenhearted and binds up their wounds." He does not offer behavior modification, but He will visit the dark, broken places of your life and make you whole.

CHAPTER 12

RIGHT AS RAIN

THE POPULAR IDIOM "right as rain" first appeared in the late 1800s.[1] The origination of the phrase is not certain, but the meaning can be interpreted as wholeness, soundness, and complete peace. The longer you live, the more you understand the priceless value of peace. You thought the cry on the inside of you was for happiness but later discovered your real thirst was for peace.

The pursuit of right as rain has you falling in and out of relationships and leaves you disappointed when money, notoriety, and success do not satisfy your inward desire for serenity. The brokenness that has invaded your life through insurmountable calamity and hurt makes a life that is right as rain seem unimaginable. You feel like you have been following a faulty GPS. You keep arriving at addresses that are not your desired destination. The reconfiguring is exhausting and draining your hope. It leaves you asking the question, "Is the life that is right as rain nothing more than utopia?"

The message of Jesus brings good news that there is a life designed for you that is right as rain. Your journey has been long with a road filled with potholes and dead end streets, but as you tune in to His GPS for your life, you will arrive at the desired destination that is right as rain.

Do not be disillusioned by your troubles. Instead, be

like the Shunammite woman in 2 Kings 4:8–36. The lesson that can be learned from her story is that wholeness does not mean that you live in a perfect world and will never experience struggles and pain, but that you *can* control how you let traumatic situations affect you. Like Abraham and Sarah, the Shunammite woman and her husband were blessed later in life with the miracle birth of a son. When the son was older, he came home early from working in the fields with his father, complaining that his head was hurting. The issue was severe, and he died in his mother's arms. The way that she confronted this calamity showed evidence that she was right as rain. When what you love dies in your arms, it is painful and causes grief. Your humanity takes over, but your calamity does not have to have the same ill effects on you as other traumatic events before. Don't build walls to isolate yourself. Don't become bitter with unforgiveness. Don't allow envy and resentment to overtake you. Don't give up; refuse to move to the potter's field and forsake your purpose. The Shunammite woman provides an illustration of how people who are right as rain respond to trauma and calamity.

She fields the questions of concern about her emotional condition from her husband and Elisha's servant in an interesting way. Her response to her brokenness is intriguing. She was not in a state of denial, but there are several notable mentions in the life of this noble woman. First, she says, "It is well" (v. 26, KJV): "I am right as rain." She meant that she was whole and at peace with the situation. She had peace because she knew she served a God who could be trusted no matter what the outcome. Second, she was a woman who understood that she was to take responsibility. Trusting God did not mean that she could sit down and do nothing. Like her, you must contribute to and have investment in your wholeness.

SHALOM

I received an e-mail from a young man that was on the journey from brokenness to wholeness. Early in his life he had experienced a lot of pain and hurt. Rejection that he received from his father filled his heart with anger and resentment. As a teenager he attempted to satisfy his brokenness with drugs and alcohol, a poorly chosen attempt to silence his raging anger. He would soon surrender his life to Jesus and discover a grace and a love like he had never known.

Over time, in his new relationship and walk with God, he grew discouraged with the dysfunctional thinking and behaviors that remained resident in his life. The discouragement was from the warfare between his carnal nature and the Holy Spirit who was confronting the issues and ill effects that resulted from his calamity and brokenness.

He had surrendered the drugs and alcohol, but it was the inward enemies that were proving to be much more stubborn and resistant. The insecurities and fear had leached to his emotions. The rejection and lack of trust was a constant hurdle to his faith. He found it challenging to trust and depend on a heavenly Father while his earthly father had brought such pain and rejection. You, like this young man, have arrived at the place where you realize you're a Christian and your past is forgiven and behind you, but you must still identify and confront the broken places that contribute to your dysfunction.

At the conclusion of the young man's e-mail he asked the question, "What does wholeness and right like rain look like?" After much thought, my response was that wholeness and a life that is right like rain is not perfection or problem free. It's not that you will never have another problem or struggle. Wholeness does not mean that you will never fail or sin again or that you will never again be challenged by your dysfunction brought to you by the painful broken places in your life. Like the Shunammite woman, it does not mean that you are never to hurt or experience pain.

It is interesting that the Hebrew word *shalom* is not limited to greetings of hello and goodbye. Shalom is defined as wholeness that is found in peace with and in God and with yourself.[2] Wholeness is what is in you as you live in a broken world. Right as rain is when you have a peace with God and in God and a peace with yourself—shalom.

PEACE WITH GOD

My wife and I purchased a house that was in need of repairs. We were drawn to the house by the potential we saw despite the fact that there was damage and decay. With commitment and an investment, what we envisioned in the house would become a reality. Before the restoration of the house could begin, we signed a contract for the purchase which was then followed by a closing. With ownership of the house and inventory of what needed to be repaired, the restoration began. It did not take long and the house was prepared and ready to become a home. We now enjoy the blessing of our new home, accompanied with the required maintenance which allows us to enjoy the full potential of what was purchased.

Jesus saw great potential in you, despite you being broken and deplorable. You were condemned and considered unworthy of occupancy. He saw in you what others, including yourself, could not see. He considered you worthy of the investment of His own blood. With ownership of what He had redeemed, the restoration of what is damaged in you began. In Psalm 23:3 King David says, "He restores my soul" (NKJV). David is speaking of the process of healing and wholeness that comes to a man that is broken and separated from God. Jesus through His blood makes the purchase, and there is peace with God (Rom. 5:1).

In a previous chapter, I mentioned that the song of the

broken is "I Still Haven't Found What I'm Looking For" by Bono of the alternative rock group U2. That being said, the song of the redeemed and of those who have found wholeness is "No Longer Slaves" by Jonathan and Melissa Helser of Bethel music. Because of Jesus and His finished work on the cross you are no longer a slave to your brokenness. You are delivered and liberated from the enemies that enslaved and held you captive. You have a new song; it is a song of freedom as your fears, shame, and every insecurity are drowned in His perfect love.

PEACE WITH YOURSELF

It is the regenerating work of grace where you receive the advantageous exchange of the ashes of your brokenness for the beauty of His wholeness. It is the ashes of your calamity and brokenness that you have difficulty releasing. It wars against having peace with yourself. You will find that professing peace to yourself will be difficult. You will need to show the same amount of grace to yourself as was shown to you in your peace with God.

Mephibosheth was from the royal family; he was the grandson of King Saul and the son of David's beloved friend Jonathan. In 2 Samuel 9:3–4, we read that David, now king, to honor his commitment and allegiance to Jonathan, inquires if there are any descendants from the house of Saul. The message came to David that Jonathan's son Mephibosheth was a resident in the barren land of Lo Debar (the dwelling for the broken and rejected). Lo Debar is where calamity displaces men and women that have lost their self-worth and have become incapacitated.

We read in 2 Samuel 4:4 that as a young man Mephibosheth was dropped by his nurse, and he did not get back up. From the fall he was damaged and broken and lame in both legs. The crippling effect in his life incapacitated not only his ability to walk but his identity and self-worth. His brokenness relocated him to the barren land of Lo Debar. King David, aware of his adversity and affliction, summoned Mephibosheth to the palace. From obscurity and poverty he is redeemed to sit at the king's table. It would be peace with himself that would hinder the peace with the king and the receiving of the provision from the king's table.

Mephibosheth was in the palace, in the presence of the king, but he was not right like rain. In 2 Samuel 9:8 he would say to King David, "What is your servant, that you should notice a dead dog like me?" The Jews considered dogs repulsive, and anything dead was considered unclean. Mephibosheth was saying, "I'm dirt, I'm an embarrassment, I'm not who I was. I don't belong here," revealing that he had peace with the king but was at war with himself. It would be much more difficult getting Lo Debar out of him then it was getting him out of Lo Debar. To obtain peace with himself, the Lo Debar mentality would have to be defeated in his life.

King David's commitment is without question; he says, "I will restore to you all the land that belonged to your grandfather Saul" (v. 7). David was indicating that he was going to reconstruct and renew his history. King David told Mephibosheth, "You will always eat at my table" (v. 7), meaning he would become as one of his sons. Being a son was something that he had forsaken and forgotten. At the age of five his father was killed in battle, and his grandfather would take his own life on the same day (1 Sam. 31:2–6). Now he is being promised sonship by the king; will the Lo Debar mentality allow him the benefits of a son? It would be the faithful kindness of the king that would allow Mephibosheth to regain his self-worth, value, and peace with himself (2 Sam. 9:13).

The father of the Prodigal in Luke 15, like King David, would illustrate the commitment to the wholeness of a son. The father declared, "[My son] was lost and is found" (v. 24). It would be the Lo Debar mentality of the son in the stink of the pig pen that would request the lodging and wages of a servant (v. 19), but the father responded and would not hear of such a request. The father declared:

> "Quick! Bring the best robe and put it on him. Put a ring on his finger and sandals on his feet. Bring the fattened calf and kill it. Let's have a feast and celebrate. For this son of mine was dead and is alive again; he was lost and is found." So they began to celebrate.
>
> —LUKE 15:22–23

It would be the love and commitment of the father that would secure the identity of the son which would solidify the peace made with himself.

As wholeness comes to what was broken in you from the calamity in your life, you will enjoy the benefits of peace with God that inaugurates wholeness and peace with yourself. Peace with God and a peace with yourself will enable the solace of the peace of God.

PEACE OF GOD

It is the life that has surrendered completely and can trust God not only with the purchase and the restoration of what was broken but also with a faith and confidence that does not revert to your emotions to determine how you respond to future calamity. It is a peace that believes "all things work together for good to those who love God, to those who are called according to His purpose" (Rom. 8:28, NKJV). It is "the peace of God, which transcends all understanding, [and] will guard your hearts and your minds in Christ Jesus" (Phil. 4:7).

The Apostle Paul is talking about a peace that transcends beyond your limits and out of the range of your ability; a peace that exposes the fear and insecurities that once dominated you in your broken state; a peace that allows for expectation of how God is going to work the calamity for your good knowing that He is able to do exceedingly abundantly above all that we ask or think (Eph. 3:20). He's talking about a peace that guards your heart and mind from the Lo Debar mentality; a peace that no matter what you encounter it is well with your soul. It was this same peace that the noble Shunammite woman had in her life as she was confronted with great loss and pain. It was the peace that Horatio Spafford had in his life as he penned the words to the song "It Is Well with My Soul" in the midst of one of the darkest days of his life.

Horatio G. Spafford was a successful lawyer and businessman in Chicago. Of his many accomplishments, there was nothing he was more grateful for than his family. He and his wife, Anna, a woman that he loved deeply, were blessed with five beautiful children. The Spaffords enjoyed life and family together. Though they cherished many memories, they were not strangers to tears and brokenness. In 1871 their son died from pneumonia and their office where they operated their business in Chicago burned to the ground. The office would reopen and the business would continue to thrive but the loss of their son would leave a void and hurt that was inconceivable.

It was on November 21, 1873, just two years after burying their son and their business burning to the ground, that the Spaffords would encounter a tragedy that would usher pain and brokenness that no family could possibly ever prepare for. Horatio, Anna, and their four girls had planned a trip to Europe, but due to an unexpected issue at work he would have to remain in Chicago with plans to meet up with his family in a few days.[3]

On November 21, 1873, the French ocean liner *Ville du Havre*, while crossing the Atlantic from the United States to Europe with 313 passengers on board, including Anna and the four children, collided with a Scottish ship. Within twelve minutes the *Ville du Havre* sank beneath the dark waters of the Atlantic. Annie, Margaret Lee, Bessie, and Tanetta, the four daughters of the Spaffords, along with 226 other passengers, did not survive the tragedy.[4]

A sailor spotted a woman floating on a piece of the wreckage. It was Anna, still alive. She was rescued and as the boat pulled away she could only stare at the waters that had taken her four daughters. She was taken to Cardiff, Wales. Anna wired her husband a message which said, "Saved alone, what shall I do?" Horatio later framed the telegram and placed it in his office.[5]

He got on the next ship to join his grieving wife. On the journey the captain would call for Horatio and tell him they were over the place where the ship went down. Horatio took a few minutes to be alone as he looked out over the waters that caused such pain and brokenness in his life. He began to write the song "It Is Well with My Soul": "When sorrows like sea billows roll, / Whatever my lot, thou hast taught me to say, / It is well, it is well with my soul." Horatio Spafford not only had peace with God, but he had a peace in God.[6]

Wholeness is allowing the Holy Spirit to touch and heal every broken place in your life. It is having a peace in knowing that no matter what you may encounter, you are in His hands. It does not mean that you are problem free or even struggle free, but there is a peace in knowing that He is with you and working in you. It is not that we go searching for calamity, but it is comforting to know that we have the peace of God if and when it is needed.

Charles Greenaway

Charles Greenaway was living in Elba, Alabama, where he and his wife were the pastors of a small church. Their nine-year-old son Daniel was sick and was not getting better but rather getting worse as his frail little body grew weaker and weaker. Charles's wife pulled him aside one day and asked him to pray that God would either heal Daniel or take him home; she couldn't stand to see him suffer. They prayed together and then Charles had to leave to take care of some things at the church.[7]

We can imagine the scene of what happened next. When Charles got home and he walked into their humble little house, sitting over in the corner by the window in the rocking chair was his wife with Daniel cradled in her arms. As he looked across the room, the moonlight shone through and was casting a glare reflecting the tears in her eyes. As their eyes met she uttered the words, "Charles, God took him."

Later that night he got alone for a time of prayer and thanked God for Daniel and the blessing he had been to his life and to their family. He pondered why God had not healed his son. His prayer continued as he said to God, "I will not go to hell over a mystery!"[8] What Greenaway was saying was, "God, I don't know why You didn't heal Daniel, but I'm going to trust You. I have a peace knowing that You are a good God; and while I may not understand, I'm going to trust You."

Charles Greenaway was a man that God used to reach the nations. Greenaway would go on to preach in some of the largest churches in America, pioneer seventeen thousand churches and thirteen Bible colleges, and preach on every continent of the world except Antarctica.[9]

Wholeness is a peace that comes from knowing God in an intimate and personal relationship. Wholeness is peace with yourself that comes from sitting at the King's table, allowing His faithful kindness to nullify the Lo Debar mentality that created your greatest foe, the enemy in you. Wholeness is the peace of God that has the ability to see what others cannot, the aptitude to see not only the enemy approaching but also to see a God that is greater and that is *for* you and a peace that transcends the range of your natural ability.

SCAR RELEASE

On May 31, 2013, twenty-three-year-old Cody Byrns was stopped at a red light on the highway when a delivery truck, which failed to stop, crashed into him from behind. Cody's vehicle exploded on impact and was engulfed in flames, leaving him trapped inside of what was left of the vehicle. The emergency responders on the scene had ruled Cody a fatality and had called the coroner's office. By a miracle, one of the responders saw his hand move and they began to cut through the twisted metal to remove his body.[10] He was air-lifted to the burn unit in Indianapolis, Indiana. He was in critical condition with 37 percent of his body burned. For three weeks Cody was on full life support and would spend two and half months in the burn unit. In his journey to recovery, he has had fourteen surgeries and months of physical therapy.

As I was talking with Cody he spoke of a procedure called a scar release; he has had six of these surgical procedures to date. He explained that when a wound begins to heal and scar, oftentimes you will lose mobility from the tightening of the skin that has scarred. The procedure complements the healing of the scar by releasing the skin that has tightened, giving back to the individual the mobility and range that had been lost.

When you begin to heal from the calamity and trauma that has come to your life, often there are emotional scars that appear. A scar is an indicator that you are healed from what has occurred that brought such pain and dysfunction to your life; but, as it was with Cody, oftentimes there is mobility and range that has been lost. You have survived the devastation but have suffered valuable losses. You have lost your joy and peace. Your dreams and passions have been lost in the aftermath of the wreck that hit your life. You vacated Lo Debar, but your self-worth and esteem have not been recovered.

Wholeness is when a scar release comes to what has been healed in your life, releases back everything that was misplaced and taken from you in your brokenness, and restores your mobility and range to dream and carry vision. David, after sitting on the ashes of Ziklag and accounting for everything that had been taken and lost in his life, rides into the camp of the Amalekites and not only defeats his enemies but recovers everything that had been taken (1 Sam. 31:1–4, 18–19). This is what Jesus was saying to the man at the pool of Bethesda: "I don't want to just heal you but I want to make you whole; I want to restore and release back unto you everything that thirty-eight years of brokenness has seized."

In wholeness, God is awakening your dream and passion, redeeming your joy and hope, and reviving your ministry that you thought would never return. Through wholeness, there is a new awareness of your value and self-worth that is coming to your life.

YOU GET TO COLOR

We have failed to see the beauty that is in the imperfections of the painting. You have submitted that your brokenness has disqualified you from the race, that God could not use someone like you. You have given up your seat at the table and feel unworthy to sit next to the likes of Absalom; you feel like you are not even in the same league as him. You hide your lameness under the skirt of the table and fail to realize that the King knew you were broken when you were invited. What you don't know is that everyone at the table is limping from something. Mephibosheth was hiding his lameness under the cloth of the table but Absalom's lameness would be revealed at the gate as he stood in betrayal of his father. (See 2 Samuel 15–19.)

Bishop Dale Bronner was spending time with his granddaughter. He was watching as she was coloring. A short time into dinner he noticed that she had stopped coloring and her little eyes were swelling up with tears. She told her grandfather that her crayon was broken and she couldn't finish the picture she was coloring. Bishop Bonner reached down and picked up the broken crayon and demonstrated for his granddaughter as he said, "Look baby, broken crayons still color."[11] The message is that you still get to color. As you are on this journey from brokenness to wholeness, dismiss the deception that you are disqualified because of the brokenness in your life. Always remember that the Bible was written by men with broken crayons. No matter where you are in the journey, keep coloring. The painting you started is waiting for you to pick up the brush and finish the portrait that lets the world know you have been here.

NOTES

INTRODUCTION

1. Mark Rutland, "10 Things I Wish I'd Known When I Was 21," accessed December 28, 2016, http://www.charismamag.com/spirit/spiritual-growth/9158-10-things-i-wish-id-known-when-i-was-21.

2. "Marcus Tullius Cicero > Quotes > Quotable Quote," *Goodreads Inc*, accessed December 28, 2016, http://www.goodreads.com/quotes/33210-a-nation-can-survive-its-fools-and-even-the-ambitious.

CHAPTER 1
THE DARK SIDE

1. "Moon" from "Pudd'nhead Wilson's New Calendar" in *Following the Equator, Twainquotes.com*, accessed December 28, 2016, http://www.twainquotes.com/Moon.html.

2. Michael Gallucci, "The Day 'The Dark Side of the Moon' Ended Its Record Chart Run," *Ultimate Classic Rock*, accessed December 28, 2016, http://ultimateclassicrock.com/dark-side-of-the-moon-ends-chart-run/.

3. Abby Ohlheiser, "NASA Gives Us an Amazing Look at the 'Dark' Side of the Moon," *The Washington Post*, February 9, 2015, https://www.washingtonpost.com/news/speaking-of-science/wp/2015/02/09/nasa-gives-us-an-amazing-look-at-the-dark-side-of-the-moon/?utm_term=.1eb6ba862e23.

CHAPTER 2
PURPOSE IN PAIN

1. "Viktor E. Frankl > Quotes > Quotable Quote," *Goodreads Inc*, accessed December 28, 2016, http://www.goodreads.com/quotes/55188-in-some-ways-suffering-ceases-to-be-suffering-at-the.

2.   "C. S. Lewis > Quotes > Quotable Quote," *Goodreads Inc*, accessed December 28, 2016, http://www.goodreads.com/ quotes/422155-mental-pain-is-less-dramatic-than-physical-pain-but-it.

3.   "Life and Work," *Viktor Frankl Institute*, accessed January 5, 2017, http://www.viktorfrankl.org/e/lifeandwork. html.

4.   Viktor Frankl, *Man's Search for Meaning* (Boston, MA: Beacon Press, 2006).

5.   Michelle Bryner, "How Do Oysters Make Pearls?" *Live Science*, November 20, 2012, http://www.livescience.com/32289-how-do-oysters-make-pearls.html.

6.   Tim Hansel, *Holy Sweat* (Waco, TX: Word, Inc., 1987), 134.

7.   Victor Goertzel and Mildred Goertzel, *Cradles of Eminence* (Boston: Little & Brown, 1962).

8.   Hansel, *Holy Sweat*.

9.   Ray Vander Laan, "Gethsemane and the Olive Press," That the World May Know, *Focus on the Family*, accessed January 5, 2017, https://www.thattheworldmayknow.com/ gethsemane-and-the-olive-press.

10.   Rick Warren, *The Purpose Driven Life: What on Earth Am I Here For?* (Grand Rapids, MI: Zondervan, 2002).

11.   Elisa Morgan, *The Beauty of Broken* (Nashville, TN: W Publishing Group, 2013).

12.   Ibid.; Elisa Morgan, *Christian Parenting Today* (May/ June 1999): 64.

13.   Frankl, *Man's Search for Meaning*.

14.   Tom Leonard, "The Man Every Woman in the World Was Just a Little Bit in Love With," *Daily Mail*, July 20, 2014, http://www.dailymail.co.uk/tvshowbiz/article-2699508/A-man-woman-world-just-little-bit-love-He-Hollywoods-amiable-star-James-Garners-brutal-childhood-gave-core-steel.html.

15.   Ibid.

16. "Write Yourself a Check," *CBN*, accessed January 31, 2017, http://www1.cbn.com/700club/write-yourself-check.

17. "Jim Carrey Net Worth," *BornRich*, accessed January 31, 2017, http://www.bornrich.com/jim-carrey.html.

18. "C. S. Lewis > Quotes > Quotable Quote," *Goodreads Inc*, accessed December 29, 2016, http://www.goodreads.com/quotes/1180-pain-insists-upon-being-attended-to-god-whispers-to-us.

CHAPTER 3
TEAR DOWN THESE WALLS

1. "Ronald Reagan 'Tear Down this Wall,'" Great Speeches Collection, *The History Place*, accessed December 29, 2016, http://www.historyplace.com/speeches/reagan-tear-down.htm.

2. "1989: Berliners Celebrate the Fall of the Wall," On This Day, *BBC*, accessed December 29, 2016, http://news.bbc.co.uk/onthisday/hi/dates/stories/november/9/newsid_2515000/2515869.stm.

3. "What Is the Origin of the 'Sticks and Stones' Quote?" *Reference .com*, accessed December 29, 2016, https://www.reference.com/education/origin-sticks-stones-quote-9d19de5da2d342a6.

4. "Ronald Reagan 'Tear Down this Wall.'"

5. "John Buchan Quotes," AZ Quotes, accessed December 29, 2016, http://www.azquotes.com/author/2105-John_Buchan.

6. Hildegard Brothers, *And I Didn't Look Back* (Bloomington, IN: Xlibris Corporation LLC, 2011).

7. "USA Life Expectancy," Measures of America 2013–2014, *World Health Ratings*, accessed January 5, 2017, http://www.worldlifeexpectancy.com/usa/life-expectancy-male.

8. "Wonder of the Day #1272; How Many Times Does Your Heart Beat in a Lifetime?" *Wonderopolis*, accessed January 5, 2017, http://wonderopolis.org/wonder/how-many-times-does-your-heart-beat-in-a-lifetime.

9.   Strong's Concordance, s.v. "compassion," http://
biblehub.com/greek/4697.htm.

10.   J. D. Bindenagel, "The Breach of the Berlin Wall," *The
Globalist*, November 8, 2014, http://www.theglobalist.com/the-
breach-of-the-berlin-wall/.

11.   "The Berlin Wall: The Fall of the Wall," Berlin Wall,
History, accessed January 6, 2017, http://www.history.com/
topics/cold-war/berlin-wall.

12.   "The Holy of Holies and the Veil," *The Tabernacle
Place*, accessed January 6, 2017, http://the-tabernacle-place.com/
articles/what_is_the_tabernacle/tabernacle_holy_of_holies.

13.   G. J. Goldberg, "The Veil of the Temple," Additions
to Josephus Reader Mail, Flavius Josephus, accessed January 6,
2017, http://josephus.org/FlJosephus3/MailAndFAQNew.htm.

14.   David Levy, *The Tabernacle* (Bellmawr, NJ: Friends of
Israel Gospel Ministry, 1993), 63.

15.   "Ben Franklin Quotes," *Brainy Quote,* accessed
December 29, 2016, https://www.brainyquote.com/quotes/
authors/b/benjamin_franklin.html.

CHAPTER 4
REINFORCED WALLS

1.   "Berlin Wall," History, *A&E Television Networks,
LLC*, accessed March 10, 2017, http://www.history.com/topics/
cold-war/berlin-wall.

2.   Quinn Myers, "The 5 Most Inescapable Prisons in the
World," *Maxim Media*, October 22, 2013, http://www.maxim.
com/maxim-man/5-most-inescapable-prisons-world.

3.   "Henry Ford > Quotes," *Goodreads Inc*, accessed
December 29, 2016, https://www.goodreads.com/author/
quotes/203714.Henry_Ford.

4.   Bruce Lowitt, "'Wrong Way' Riegels Takes off into
History," *St. Petersburg Times*, September 26, 1999, http://www.
sptimes.com/News/92699/news_pf/Sports/_Wrong_Way__
Riegels_t.shtml.

5. Dan O'Sullivan, "1902—Michigan 49, Stanford 0," *ESPN*, December 13, 2002, http://www.espn.com/abcsports/bcs/rose/s/1902.html.

6. Lowitt, "'Wrong Way' Riegels."

7. Ibid.

8. *Wikipedia*, s.v. "Roy Riegels," last modified December 27, 2016, https://en.wikipedia.org/wiki/Roy_Riegels.

9. Lowitt, "'Wrong Way' Riegels."

10. Ibid.

11. Ibid.

12. "Roy Riegels, 84, Who Took Off in Wrong Direction in Rose Bowl," Obituaries, *The New York Times*, March 28, 1993, http://www.nytimes.com/1993/03/28/obituaries/roy-riegels-84-who-took-off-in-wrong-direction-in-rose-bowl.html.

13. Benny Hsu, "Famous People Who Found Success Despite Failure," *Get busy Living* (blog), http://getbusylivingblog.com/famous-people-who-found-success-despite-failures/.

14. Ibid.

15. Kellie Van Gilder, "The Story Behind Billy Graham's First Sermon," *Billy Graham Evangelistic Association*, July 18, 2014, accessed January 31, 2017, https://billygraham.org/story/the-story-behind-billy-grahams-first-sermon/.

16. "Billy Graham's Ministries Have Reached More Than 2 Billion People," *FilmRise* (blog), January 4, 2017, http://filmrise.com/billy-grahams-ministries-have-reached-more-than-2-billion-people-see-why-in-gathering-of-souls-the-billy-graham-crusades/.

17. "Billy Graham: Evangelist to Millions," Christian History, *Christianity Today*, http://www.christianitytoday.com/history/people/evangelistsandapologists/billy-graham.html.

18. Ibid.

19. "Billy Graham's Ministries Have Reached More Than 2 Billion People."

20. "Bio: Tony Dungy," *Biography.com*, accessed December 29, 2016, http://www.biography.com/people/tony-dungy-21330527#personal-life.

21. Ibid.

22. Ibid.

23. Kevin Bowen, "Looking Back: October 6:2003," Indianapolis Colts, *Colts, Inc.*, accessed March 15, 2017, http://www.colts.com/news/article-1/LOOKING-BACK--OCTOBER-6-2003/8fd2c4cd-eafc-424d-ad37-2b924363fe06.

24. Ibid.

25. Skip Wood, "In Your Dreams? Colts Pull It Off," *USA Today*, October 8, 2003, accessed December 29, 2016, http://usatoday30.usatoday.com/sports/football/nfl/colts/2003-10-08-colts-comeback_x.htm.

CHAPTER 5
SCARLET LETTER

1. Nathaniel Hawthorne, *The Scarlet Letter* (London: Vintage Classic, 2008).

2. Joel Kilpatrick, "He Dares to Give Love," *Charisma Magazine*, http://www.charismamag.com/spirit/devotionals/loving-god?view=article&id=850:he-dares-to-give-love&catid=146.

3. Ibid.

4. Hawthorne, *The Scarlet Letter*.

5. Max Lucado, *No Wonder They Call Him the Savior* (Nashville, TN: Thomas Nelson, 2004).

6. Herbert Mitgang, "Sealed with Sorrow: Mary Lincoln in Letters," *The New York Times*, September 9, 1999, http://www.nytimes.com/1999/09/09/arts/sealed-with-sorrow-mary-lincoln-in-letters.html.

7. Ibid.

8. Ibid.

9. Cath Martin, "Jackie Kennedy after JFK's Assassination: 'I'm So Bitter Against God,'" *World, Christianity*

Today, May 14, 2014, http://www.christiantoday.com/article/ jackie.kennedy.after.jfks.assassination.../37431.htm.

10. Carl Anthony, "The Children of Jacqueline Kennedy," *National First Ladies' Library* (blog), September 19, 2013, accessed January 31, 2017, http://www.firstladies.org/blog/the-children-of-jacqueline-kennedy/.

11. Barbara Leaming, *Jacqueline Bouvier Kennedy Onassis: The Untold Story* (New York: Thomas Dunne Books, 2014).

12. Ibid

13. Martin, "Jackie Kennedy."

14. Jeremy Bojczuk, *22 November 1963: An Introduction to the JFK Assassination* (n.p: Boxgrove Publishing, 2014).

15. Martin, "Jackie Kennedy."

16. Ibid.

17. Elizabeth Flock, "What They Found in Lincoln's Pockets the Night He Was Shot," *U.S. News* (blog), *U.S. News & World Report,* May 24, 2013, http://www.usnews.com/news/ blogs/washington-whispers/2013/05/24/what-they-found-in-lincolns-pockets-the-night-he-was-shot.

18. Nancy Brewka Clark, "Nathaniel Hawthorne's Struggle and Romance with Salem," *Literary Traveler,* July 16, 2005, http://www.literarytraveler.com/articles/hawthorne_salem_ma/.

19. "Hawthorne's Wife Saved Money for Book," *Faith Committee of the Character Council of Greater Cincinnati and Northern Kentucky,* accessed January 31, 2017, http:// www.charactercincinnati.org/Faith/Qualities/Gentleness/ hawthorneswifesaved.htm.

20. Clark, "Nathaniel Hawthorne's Struggle."

Chapter 6
Potter's Field

1. *Encyclopedia of the Bible,* s.v. "Akeldam," accessed January 9, 2017, https://www.biblegateway.com/resources/ encyclopedia-of-the-bible/Akeldama.

2. "Beate Kuhn," *Ceramics Today*, accessed January 9, 2017, http://www.ceramicstoday.com/potw/beate_kuhn.htm.

3. "Letter from John Adams to Abigail Adams, 13 April 1777," Adams Family Papers, *Massachusetts Historical Society*, accessed December 29, 2016, https://www.masshist.org/digitaladams/archive/doc?id=L17770413jasecond.

4. Ibid.

5. *It's a Wonderful Life*, by Philip Van Dorn Stern, directed by Frank Capra, 1946.

6. Eric Metaxas, "Michael Phelps Is Driven," Breakpoint, accessed December 29, 2016, http://www.breakpoint.org/bpcommentaries/entry/13/29694.

7. Ibid

8. Michelle Y Hee Lee, "Does the United States Really Have 5 Percent of the World's Population and a Quarter of the World's Prisoners?" *The Washington Post*, April 30, 2015, https://www.washingtonpost.com/news/fact-checker/wp/2015/04/30/does-the-united-states-really-have-five-percent-of-worlds-population-and-one-quarter-of-the-worlds-prisoners/?utm_term=.d502597853a7.

9. Kennedy Hickman, "World War II: Operation Pastoris," About Education, *About, Inc.*, accessed December 30, 2016, http://militaryhistory.about.com/od/socialeffectsofwar/p/pastorius.htm.

10. Tom, "Six Nazi Saboteurs Executed in Washington," Ghosts of DC, February 9, 2012, http://ghostsofdc.org/2012/02/09/six-nazi-saboteurs-executed-in-washington/.

11. Nina Bernstein, "Unearthing the Secrets of New York's Mass Graves," *New York Times*, May 15, 2015, http://www.nytimes.com/interactive/2016/05/15/nyregion/new-york-mass-graves-hart-island.html?_r=0.

12. "City Cemetery Hart Island (Potter's Field)," City of New York Correction Department, http://www.correctionhistory.org/html/chronicl/nycdoc/html/hart.html.

13. "Potter's Field," Historical Resume of Potter's Field: 1869–1967, *New York Society Correction History*, http://www.correctionhistory.org/html/chronicl/hart/html/hartbook2.html.

14. Bernstein, "Unearthing the Secrets"

15. Ibid.

16. Full story of Bobby Driscoll found at http://www.findadeath.com/Deceased/d/Bobby_Driscoll/Death_of_Bobby_driscoll.htm.

17. Ibid.

18. Kenetha Stanton, "A Kintsugi Life," accessed January 9, 2017, https://akintsugilife.com/.

CHAPTER 7
SNAKE BITTEN

1. Gregory Juckett, "Venomous Snakebites in the United States: Management Review and Update," *American Family Physician*, April 1, 2002, http://www.aafp.org/afp/2002/0401/p1367.html.

2. "U. S. and World Population Clock," *United States Census Bureau*, accessed December 30, 2016, http://www.census.gov/popclock/.

3. Iakhovas, "Top 10 Most Venomous Snakes," *Listverse*, March 30, 2011, accessed December 30, 2016, http://listverse.com/2011/03/30/top-10-most-venomous-snakes/.

4. Ibid.

5. Cobra Master, "Philippine Cobra: Deadliest on the Planet?" *Cobras.org*, November 6, 2014, http://cobras.org/philippine-cobra/.

6. Alan Carr, "Living Above the Snake Line," The Sermon Notebook, accessed December 30, 2016, http://www.sermonnotebook.org/new%20testament/Colossians%201_9-17.htm.

7. "Ben Carson Biography," Bio, *Biography.com*, accessed December 30, 2016, http://www.biography.com/people/ben-carson-475422#separating-conjoined-twins.

8. "Ben Carson," *National Review*, accessed December 30, 2016, http://www.nationalreview.com/author/ben-carson.

9. Ben Carson, "My Personal Relationship With God," *FaithGateway*, accessed January 9, 2017, http://www.faithgateway.com/ben-carson-personal-relationship-god/#.WHQg1RsrLIU

10. Ben Carson's Facebook page, accessed January 9, 2017, https://www.facebook.com/drbencarson/photos/a.845905202190986.1073741828.686786988102809/922103801237792/.

11. "Johnny Cash Biography," Bio, *Biography.com*, accessed December 30, 2016, http://www.biography.com/people/johnny-cash-9240610#synopsis.

12. Ibid.

13. Ibid.

14. Ibid.

15. Ibid.

16. Johnny Cash, *Man in White* (Nashville, TN: Westbow Press, 2006).

17. "Johnny Cash Biography."

18. Jerry Walls, "The World's Deadliest Snakes," *Reptiles*, accessed December 30, 2016, http://www.reptilesmagazine.com/Snakes/Wild-Snakes/The-Worlds-Deadliest-Snakes/.

19. Cobra Master, "Philippine Cobra."

CHAPTER 8
COLLATERAL DAMAGE

1. "Hurricane Andrew: 20 Facts You May Have Forgotten," *The Huffington Post*, August 24, 2012, http://www.huffingtonpost.com/2012/08/21/20-facts-hurricane-andrew-anniversary_n_1819405.html.

2. Ibid.

3. Libin V. Babu, "Speech on Psalms 27," *Welcome to the World of Creativity* (blog), September 26, 2010, http://libinvbabu.blogspot.com/2010/09/speech-on-psalms-27.html.

4.   Max Lucado quoted in Daniel Hill, *10-10: Life to the Fullest* (Grand Rapids, MI: Baker Books, 2014).

5.   John Wesley, "Beliefnet's Inspirational Quotes," *Beliefnet*, accessed January 31, 2016, http://www.beliefnet.com/quotes/evangelical/j/john-wesley/give-me-one-hundred-preachers-who-fear-nothing-but.aspx#tpDFCKBMAHgIpLSh.99.

6.   "Edmund Burke Quotes," Brainy Quote, accessed January 4, 2017, https://www.brainyquote.com/quotes/quotes/e/edmundburk382368.html.

7.   "Wild West Outlaws and Lawmen: Black Bart," *thewildwest.org*, accessed January 31, 2017, http://www.thewildwest.org/cowboys/wildwestoutlawsandlawmen/173-blackbart.

8.   "10 Interesting Facts About Benjamin Harrison," *Republicanpresidents.com*, accessed January 4, 2017, http://www.republicanpresidents.net/10-interesting-facts-about-benjamin-harrison/.

9.   Max Lucado, *The Applause of Heaven* (Nashville, TN: Thomas Nelson, 1999), 82.

10.   "Alfred Hitchcock > Quotes > Quotable Quote," *Goodreads Inc*, accessed January 4, 2017, http://www.goodreads.com/quotes/449460-i-m-frightened-of-eggs-worse-than-frightened-they-revolt-me.

11.   Alexander Armstrong and Richard Osman, "How Hitler Was Terrified by Pussycats..." *Daily Mail*, April 25, 2014, http://www.dailymail.co.uk/femail/article-2612195/How-Hitler-terrified-pussycats-perfectly-Pointless-trivia.html.

12.   "Johnny Depp Explains Why He Is Afraid of Clowns," Film Rise, accessed January 4, 2017, http://filmrise.com/johnny-depp-explains-why-he-is-afraid-of-clowns/.

13.   "Florence Chadwick 1953–1964," Queen of the Channel, *Channel Swimming Association*, accessed January 4, 2017, http://www.queenofthechannel.com/florence-chadwick.

14.   Randy Alcorn, "Florence Chadwick and the Fog," *Eternal Perspective Ministries* (blog), January 21, 2010, http://www.epm.org/resources/2010/Jan/21/florence-chadwick-and-fog/.

15.   "Florence Chadwick 1953–1964."

16.   Will Swanton and Fred Pawle, "Surfer Mick Fanning Survives Shark Attack at South Africa's J-Bay Final," *The Australian*, July 20, 2015, http://www.theaustralian.com.au/sport/surfer-mick-fanning-survives-shark-attack-at-south-africas-jbay-final/news-story/da00eff1f50d31f3fd7006a28b34f402.

17.   "Mick Fanning Wins on Return to Scene of Shark Attack at J-Bay Open," *The Guardian*, Australian Associated Press, July 6, 2016, https://www.theguardian.com/sport/2016/jul/06/mick-fanning-wins-on-return-to-scene-of-shark-attack-at-j-bay-open.

CHAPTER 9
THE JUDAS GOAT

1.   "The Judas Goat Phenomenon," *Historeo.com*, accessed January 10, 2017, http://historeo.com/web/?p=136.

2.   Frankl, *Man's Search for Meaning.*

3.   "Alexander Hamilton and His Patron, George Washington," People & Events, Alexander Hamilton, *American Experience*, accessed January 10, 2017, http://www.pbs.org/wgbh/amex/hamilton/peopleevents/e_washington.html.

4.   Ibid.

5.   "Bio: Alexander Hamilton," Biography.com, accessed January 10, 2017, http://www.biography.com/people/alexander-hamilton-9326481#synopsis.

6.   *Rocky* (1976), by Sylvester Stallone, directed by John Avildsen, http://www.imdb.com/title/tt0075148/.

7.   *Rocky III* (1982), by Sylvester Stallone, directed by Sylvester Stallone, http://www.imdb.com/title/tt0084602/quotes.

8.   *Rocky Balboa* (2006), by Sylvester Stallone, directed by Sylvester Stallone, http://www.imdb.com/title/tt0479143/quotes.

9.   Movie Encyclopedia, s.v. "Sylvester Stallone," http://movieencyclopedia.tripod.com/sylvesterstallonebiography.htm.

10.   Vashnu Verma, "Sylvester Stallone's Success Story Will Inspire You to Pursue Your Dreams," *Calling Dreams* (blog), September 23, 2014, http://callingdreams.com/success-story-of-sylvester-stallone/.

CHAPTER 10
ORPHAN SPIRIT

1.   Adena Andrews, "6 Best Riley Curry Postgame News Conference Moments," *ESPN*,

2.   May 28, 2015, http://www.espn.com/espnw/athletes-life/article/12967618/6-best-riley-curry-postgame-press-conference-moments.

CHAPTER 11
JOURNEY TO WHOLENESS

1.   "Joni Eareckson Tada on Something Greater than Healing," interview by Sarah Pulliam Bailey, *Christianity Today*, October 8, 2010, http://www.christianitytoday.com/ct/2010/october/12.30.html; Joni Eareckson, "A Victory Through Suffering," *Power to Change Ministries*, accessed January 31, 2017, https://powertochange.com/discover/faith/jeareckson/.

2.   Ibid.

3.   Ibid.

4.   "LeMessurier Stands Strong: A Case Study in Professional Ethics," *AIA Trust*, accessed January 11, 2017, http://www.theaiatrust.com/whitepapers/ethics/study.php.

5.   Evan Andrews, "The Assassination of President James Garfield," *History in the Headlines*, July 1, 2016, http://www.history.com/news/the-assassination-of-president-james-a-garfield.

6. Strong's Concordance, s.v. "Skandalon," http://biblehub.com/greek/4625.htm.

7. "MercyMe," *Song Facts*, accessed January 11, 2017, http://www.songfacts.com/facts-mercyme.php.

8. *Wikipedia*, s.v. "List of Awards and Nominations Received by MercyMe," last modified February 13, 2016, https://en.wikipedia.org/wiki/List_of_awards_and_nominations_received_by_MercyMe.

9. Harry Hughes, "Brooklyn Bus Ministry of Bill Wilson," *Premier*, accessed January 11, 2017, http://www.premier.org.uk/Topics/Church/Mission/The-Brooklyn-Bus-Ministry-of-Bill-Wilson.

10. Violet Nesdoly, "Jesus Glows in the Dark," *Inscribe* (blog), December 12, 2010, http://inscribewritersonline.blogspot.com/2010/12/jesus-glows-in-dark-nesdoly.html.

CHAPTER 12
RIGHT AS RAIN

1. *Dictionary.com*, s.v. "Right as Rain," http://www.dictionary.com/browse/right-as-rain.

2. "Peace—Shalom (Hebrew Word Study)," *Precept Austin*, accessed January 12, 2017, http://www.preceptaustin.org/shalom_-_definition.

3. Terry Lindsay, "Story Behind the Song: 'It is Well With My Soul,'" *The St. Augustine Record*, July 16, 2016, http://staugustine.com/living/religion/2016-07-14/story-behind-song-it-well-my-soul.

4. Ibid.

5. Ibid.

6. Ibid.

7. Perry Stone, *There's a Crack in Your Armor* (Lake Mary, FL: Charisma House, 2014), 158–159.

8. Ibid.

9. Ibid.

10. Tabitha Waggoner, "2 Injured in Fiery Crash," *Princeton Daily Clarion*, May 31, 2013, http://www.pdclarion. com/news/local_news/injured-in-fiery-crash/article_d8045ba9-0038-5b73-8f86-c43e5370ac0f.html.

11. "Broken Crayons Still Color," YouTube video, 1:17, from an interview televised by TBN, posted by Trinity Broadcasting Network, December 15, 2015, https://www.youtube.com/ watch?v=GwBZqjrukSk.

ABOUT THE AUTHOR

AUTHOR AND SPEAKER Johnny Honaker, along with his wife, CC (Cecilia), pastors a growing multicultural church in the greater Tampa Bay area. Johnny is anointed to bring a message of hope and restoration to the broken and wounded of the nations. His love and passion for people allow him to see beyond the hurt and brokenness of shattered lives to the potential and greatness in them. He is a voice of hope in the midst of what has the appearance of a hopeless situation in the lives of men and women. Johnny and CC reside in Riverview, Florida, and have two married children.

CONTACT THE AUTHOR

Johnny Honaker
River of Life Christian Center
6605 Krycul Ave
Riverview, FL 33578

Office Number: 813-677-4453, extension 329

Website: TheEnemyInYou.com